POOLS AND SPAS

by Curtis Rist, Vicky Webster,
and the Editors of Sunset Books, Menlo Park, California

SUNSET BOOKS

VICE PRESIDENT, EDITORIAL DIRECTOR: Bob Doyle
DIRECTOR OF SALES: Brad Moses
DIRECTOR OF OPERATIONS: Rosann Sutherland
MARKETING MANAGER: Linda Barker
ART DIRECTOR: Vasken Guiragossian

STAFF FOR THIS BOOK
MANAGING EDITOR: Bridget Biscotti Bradley
ART DIRECTOR: Amy Gonzalez
PHOTO EDITOR: Cynthia del Fava
COPY EDITOR: John Edmonds
PRINCIPAL ILLUSTRATOR: Tracy La Rue Hohn
PRODUCTION SPECIALIST: Linda M. Bouchard
PREPRESS COORDINATOR: Danielle Johnson
INDEXER: Nanette Cardon/IRIS

For additional copies of *Pools and Spas* or any other
Sunset book, visit us at www.sunsetbooks.com.

For more exciting home and garden ideas, visit
myhomeideas.com

contents

JUMP in

NOT SO LONG AGO, a backyard swimming pool was considered the epitome of luxury—and with good reason. Pools were expensive to install, time-consuming, and costly to maintain. As for spas, well, until the hot-tub craze swept the country in the 1970s, few people outside California had even heard of the things. In recent years, though, several trends have converged to change that picture.

a pool or spa for
EVERYONE

New products and construction techniques have made swimming pools and spas more affordable than ever. As a result, their popularity has skyrocketed, even in places where the swimming season is short.

The photo gallery on these pages is designed to both fuel your imagination and show you some of the many practical options available to would-be pool and spa owners. Our "exhibit" includes pools that are literally works of art—personal statements whose creators spared no expense in their design and construction. These are the pools to dream of. In other photos, you'll see examples of pools and spas that are modest in size and materials. In these cases, note how the surrounding landscaping can make a simple pool seem grand.

▶ A SUNSET SOAK Perched high in the trees, this spa invites you to stay a little longer and watch the sun go down.

▶ LUSH LANDSCAPING A flagstone path meandering through grasses and ground covers leads to a rectangular pool with concrete decking. While the pool itself is modest, the surrounding landscaping makes it look spectacular.

▼ LOW COUNTRY STYLE A pink wall with climbing vines and a weathered red-brick patio surrounds a simple lap pool in this South Carolina garden.

▲ WHITE AND BLUE Like white sand abutting a blue ocean, this poolside sitting area has a fresh, clean, and relaxing look.

◀ CLEAN LINES On this sloping lot, the pool connects to a deck on one side and is raised on the other. The concrete sides are tinted a warm burnt umber, adding color to the green and blue landscape.

▶ MORNING FOG Multisized limestone slabs dress up this large pool area, which has plenty of room for lounging. Tall grasses flanking a group of chairs provide privacy for sunbathing, and they break up the expanse of open space beyond.

▲ **CONSTANT MOTION**
A waterfall feeds into this L-shaped pool on one side, while spa water drifts in through a channel on the other. The large window provides an uninterrupted view of the water from inside the house.

◄ **WATER WORLD** Swirling water that flows over the edge spills into a catch basin where the pool deck dips downward, then circulates back into the pool. The effect is mesmerizing.

▶ MODERN ART A sheet of water flowing over metal accents interrupts the long white wall that runs along one side of this pool. A lounge chair and simple round planter reinforce the modern style.

▼ RAISED SPA Faced in blue and brown tiles, this raised spa with a waterfall shares the limelight with the pool.

◀ REFLECTING POOL When creating a landscape, position the plants so they'll reflect in the water. Here, it looks like there are twice as many colorful grasses and flowers as there really are.

▼ TROPICAL ELEGANCE A wrought-iron gate with concrete pillars creates a stately entrance to this pool.

14

▲ SECRET GARDEN A lap pool surrounded by wisteria, hostas, and shrubs looks like it has been there for as many decades as the cobblestone patio and walls have.

▶ NEW ENGLAND SUMMER Nothing says classic simplicity like four Adirondack chairs lined up alongside a pool amid lush grass.

◄ FIRE AND WATER When the sun sets over this desert landscape, a fire pit built over the circular, negative-edge pool lights up the night sky.

▼ NIGHT LIGHTS Underwater lights create a glowing blue oasis to gaze out on from inside the house.

▲ POOL PARTY This sweeping Arizona backyard was built for entertaining, with seating
areas for eating, lounging, and sitting by
the fire. Bright red cushions on the woven
outdoor furniture match the blooming
bougainvillea. Lights spread across the landscape and in the pool allow the party to go
late into the night.

▶ WATER JETS A little night dip is made
possible by underwater lighting in this jetted
spa. The surrounding patio is illuminated by
lights filtering through the glass doors, plus
an outdoor light on the side of the house.

17

▶ **BAMBOO WALL** The right plants can add a sculptural effect to your landscape. These trimmed bamboo stalks reflect in the water but don't hide the vine-covered fence behind them. A pot allows the citrus tree to sit closer to the water.

▼ **ISLAND BREEZE** Protect your family from the sun and add island flavor by building a thatched-roof ramada (see page 173). This colorful landscape also features palm trees and pink flowers in circular planting beds at the edges of the pool.

▲ **ANGLE TOWARD THE OCEAN** When standard shapes and sizes won't work, it's time to get creative. This angular pool was made to fit on an oddly shaped lot. The pool and spa are separated by more of the glossy stone surround, with a gurgling fountain in the middle. Hooks screw into the holes along the edges of the pool to support the pool cover.

◀ **ACCESSORIES** Instead of throwing beach towels on the ground, use them to add some style to the poolside. Here, towels are draped over an iron coat rack.

◀ VERTICAL GREEN A wall of horsetail is a striking addition to this rectangular pool. Horsetail is hardy, loves water, and doesn't drop any leaves, making it an ideal poolside plant. It is invasive, though, so keep it in pots or planters.

▲ CLASSICAL FOUNTAIN Add some art to your pool with a decorative fountain.

▶ LIVING SCULPTURES Trees with interesting branches can be lit from below to create a magical effect around a pool.

▲ STATELY PRESENCE While it needn't be as grand as this one, a pool house is a wonderful addition, particularly when the pool is a good distance from the main house. All you really need are storage space for pool supplies and a room to change into your suit. This pillared example also serves as a guesthouse.

▲ LAP POOL A variety of seating options under a vine-covered pergola offers something for everyone. Once rested, you can use the lap pool to get your heart rate back up.

▶ ENJOY THE AMBIANCE Not in the mood for a swim? You can still enjoy the pool if you have a comfortable chair or two, an ottoman to put your feet up on, and a cup of warm tea. Here, the sound of the waterfall muffles any distractions so you can read or just let your mind wander.

▶ **MOUNTAIN OASIS** Concrete that's shaped and tinted to resemble natural stone makes this spa look like something you might happen upon in nature. Palms soften the edges.

▽ **WARM DESERT GLOW** If you don't watch where you step in this backyard, you might end up in the spa. The glassy water spills over the edge and is filtered through gravel before being pumped back into the pool and spa. On chilly nights, the homeowners can ignite the fire pit next to the spa.

▲ NATURALISTIC Tucked into the corner of the yard, this free-form pool blends nicely with the surrounding landscape. A spill fountain towers over one side of the pool.

◄ YOUR CABANA OR MINE? Nothing makes you feel like you're on vacation more than lounging under a cabana in your own backyard. The drapes can be drawn as the sun shifts throughout the day.

► RINSE OFF Tucked around the corner from the pool, this outdoor shower makes it easy to rinse off before and after your daily swim. Showering amid the flowers and trees can be habit-forming—you might indulge even on days when you aren't swimming. Having a solid privacy wall like this one comes in handy when bathing suits are optional. For more on outdoor showers, see pages 174–175.

◀ **VIEW FROM AFAR** After a long day of working in the garden and doing chores around the house, relax in this raised, portable spa and enjoy the view.

▶ **ENGLISH GARDEN** French doors lead to this stone-faced spa surrounded by fragrant white roses. The wide ledge allows you to sit on the side and dip your feet in.

▲ **COLOR AND FORM** The edges of this rectangular pool are flanked with glazed evergreen pots filled with sculpted shrubs and purple flowers. Pots allow you to bring color to concrete, wood, or stone pool surrounds.

▶ **HIDDEN JEWEL** Add an air of mystery to your pool with an iron scrollwork gate. The pine trees allow only a glimpse of the cool blue water beyond.

PLANNING

A BACKYARD SWIMMING POOL used to mean an in-ground rectangle or an above-ground circle. Today there are countless design options. Spas also offer a wealth of choices, from those that can be set up in minutes to in-ground units that connect to swimming pools. But before deciding on the style, shape, and materials, consider how you will use your pool or spa, what the costs will be, where you will place it, and which contractor you will use. Let's take an in-depth look at each of these areas.

pool and spa
USES

The first consideration in planning a new pool or refurbishing an existing one is how you plan to use it. While pools can serve multiple functions, focusing on your principal needs and wants will help you choose wisely as you work on placement and positioning in your yard or home.

RECREATION

Recreation is the key reason most people build a pool. After all, who doesn't want to cool down in hot weather and have a wonderful place to while away the hours?

If your goal is spending weekends with your family in a pool filled with inflatable toys and perhaps a floating lounge chair, that might suggest you don't have to construct the most luxurious model. A lower-cost version, such as an above-ground pool, may suit you—and still leave plenty in the budget for swimming lessons.

Nor is a deep pool essential, especially if young children are involved. For example, if you want to play water volleyball and swim the occasional lap, a constant depth of 4 feet should be more than adequate—deep enough to splash and swim in yet shallow enough to provide safety for people of all ages.

EXERCISE

While splashing about in even the shallowest of pools provides some exercise, serious athletes and those looking for the therapeutic benefits of water exercise will probably want a lap pool.

A pool intended purely for exercise doesn't require extensive room around it for socializing. This lap pool makes excellent use of a long, narrow space secluded by mature shrubs.

Olympic pools are 50 meters (about 164 feet) long, but it's not necessary to build anything that size. A pool ranging from 25 to 40 feet will allow a swimmer to execute several swift butterfly or freestyle strokes before having to reverse direction. For lap swimming, a depth of 3½ feet is adequate.

For water aerobics and other forms of exercise, such as jogging with a float belt, you'll need a pool that's deep enough for you to tread water in without constantly touching the sides or the bottom—in most cases 5 or 6 feet should suffice. Likewise, if the pool is to be used for physical therapy, you may not need an overly deep one.

One excellent option for accommodating the need for exercise is a swim spa. With the flick of a button, a pump creates a powerful water current that the swimmer moves against while swimming in place. Although swim spas can be built outdoors, they can also be brought indoors thanks to their compact size (see more about swim spas on page 75).

ABOVE LEFT: One of a pool's many benefits is that kids will get good exercise while having fun.

ABOVE: A well-planned pool satisfies many needs at once. Combining good looks with manageable size, this simple pool maximizes the possibilities for safe recreation.

TO DIVE OR NOT TO DIVE

INCLUDING A DIVING BOARD or slide is a tempting option, but both raise a long list of concerns—and many pool contractors refuse to add them. To prevent injury, a pool with even a low diving board needs an area at least 9 or 10 feet deep that extends out at least 12 feet in front of the diving board. In all cases, pools with diving boards must be built according to the safe-diving specifications developed by the National Spa and Pool Institute (see "Resources" on page 234). Diving boards and slides may require additional liability insurance, and they will require more intensive supervision of children using the pool.

In many cases, a swimming pool serves as a backdrop for outdoor entertaining. Here, guests can lounge by the pool on cushioned chairs, enjoy a cheeseburger cooked in the outdoor kitchen, and keep warm by the fire as the sun goes down.

For example, you may choose not only to surround the pool with a deck or patio but also to connect it to the house for access to the kitchen and indoor bathrooms. You may also want to add structures to hide pool equipment, as well as a pool house to provide changing areas. A pool used for entertaining can grow into a much larger project.

RELAXATION AND THERAPY

Floating in a pool or sitting in a lounge chair alongside one can certainly be relaxing. An even better way to unwind is to step into a spa or hot tub. These units take two major forms: either in-ground or portable (also known as above-ground).

An in-ground spa is almost always connected directly to a swimming pool and shares the pool's water filtration and heating equipment. For a spa that won't be linked to a pool, the portable variety makes the most sense. It requires no excavation and can be located nearly anywhere, even indoors. Often, people build decking around a portable spa to give

ENTERTAINING

If hosting outdoor gatherings is factored into the mix, you'll have a few additional considerations. Not only will your pool need to function well and be an inviting and safe place for recreation, but you will want it to look exceptionally good too. While this may not alter its overall function and form, it will affect your decisions about how to approach landscaping.

it the look of an in-ground spa without doing any digging.

Because portable spas have the necessary pipes, filters, and heaters built in, setting them up is usually quick. In fact, some portable tubs truly rank as do-it-yourself projects that anyone can tackle—you simply plug them in, fill them with water, and begin soaking.

ABOVE: After a therapeutic dip in this hot tub near a roaring fire, the owners can slide the cover over the water to create a solid, low-level deck. That way, the small courtyard can be used for entertaining as well.

LEFT: This large in-ground spa has plenty of room for a party, but the idyllic setting is also conducive to solitary relaxation.

THE EFFECTS OF HOT WATER

HOT WATER FROM A SPA helps relax the body by warming muscles and causing blood vessels to dilate; the effect can be similar to having a massage. Still, spas aren't for everyone. People with heart disease or blood-pressure disorders, or women who are pregnant, should consult a physician before stepping into a spa.

calculating
THE COSTS

While swimming pools do rank as luxuries, there is a pool for almost every budget and need. Just remember to include auxiliary expenses such as maintenance and additional insurance when determining the total cost of the pool.

This in-ground gunite pool complements the design of the house, includes a spa, and has a two-tiered water feature, making the installation costs on the high end of the spectrum.

OPERATING COSTS

Operating a pool or a spa can lead to some surprising expenses, beginning with the water to fill it. Given that the average pool holds approximately 20,000 gallons of water, the cost can be considerable. If you install a water heater, you need to include fuel costs, along with the expense of electricity to operate the filtration and purification systems. Fuel and electric rates vary

A small and simple pool also made of gunite will cost less to install and can be jazzed up with colorful outdoor furniture.

TIP

COST

When you're creating a budget, one way to manage the costs is to proceed on the project in phases. Build the pool or spa first, putting basic electrical and plumbing necessities in place. Later you can upgrade by adding heaters, automatic cleaners, and lighting, as well as decks, patios, landscaping, and a pool house.

widely in different parts of the country, but, depending on your location and climate, operational costs for a pool or spa can add hundreds of dollars to your monthly utility bill.

Even if you live in a warm area of the country, it doesn't automatically mean you will have a lower overall energy bill. In Florida, for instance, it may cost more to heat a pool than it would in Illinois, because you'll be using the pool year-round rather than just four or five months a year. The best way to avoid sticker shock is to check with pool owners and pool builders in your area. Ask to see actual bills that can help you estimate what your costs might be.

INSTALLATION COSTS

While the specific costs for constructing a pool or spa vary by region as well as by season, here are some broad price guidelines. These numbers reflect minimum costs; special materials, equipment, or landscaping will raise the prices.

TYPE OF POOL	COST
Basic above-ground pool	$6,000–$8,000
Large above-ground pool with deck	$10,000–$12,000
Basic in-ground pool lined with vinyl	$18,000–$20,000
Basic in-ground pool made with gunite	$22,000–$27,000
Basic in-ground spa pool made of fiberglass	$25,000–$30,000
Rectangular lap pool	$25,000–$30,000
Gunite pool-spa combination	$30,000–$35,000
Gunite pool-spa combination with waterfall	$40,000–$45,000
Portable spa	$2,000–$4,000
Wooden hot tub	$4,000–$6,000
In-ground spa	$8,000–$10,000

MAINTENANCE COSTS

The pristine waters of a beautifully maintained swimming pool can be a delight to look at and jump into. Keeping that water looking fresh, however, takes work and a financial commitment. Without maintenance, a pool or spa will quickly become an algae-filled pond. You'll need to keep the water chemically balanced and sanitary, maintain the filtration and heating equipment, and clean the pool edges and surrounding patio or deck surfaces. As many homeowners discover, the amount of time this requires can often equal—if not exceed—the amount of time they actually spend swimming in the pool.

Advances in pool-maintenance equipment, which are discussed in chapter 8, can make the pool easier to take care of. But the initial cost of such equipment can

ABOVE: This small pool tucked into a courtyard increases the property's value, and the maintenance costs are manageable.

LEFT: Beyond basic rectangles and ovals, pools can be created in any shape imaginable. The strong geometry of this pool is an example of how striking originality can emerge from a bold plan and the simplest of materials.

easily double the price of the pool itself. Another option is to hire a pool service company to do the work for you. Either way, thinking about these expenses in advance can help you determine which size pool or spa best suits your budget as well as your needs.

LIABILITY COSTS

As much fun as they can be, pools and outdoor spas pose an additional liability risk. Most communities have zoning laws that govern safety—such as requiring fencing around the pool or having a cover in place when the pool is not in use. While these are worthwhile regulations, they entail some expense. Even something as innocuous-sounding as a fence can cost thousands of dollars to install. Your homeowners' insurance premiums are also likely to rise if you add a pool, especially the liability portions. Such costs vary widely, and the only way to accurately gauge the increase is to ask your insurance agent.

INCREASED PROPERTY VALUE

FOR MANY YEARS, swimming pools were considered a liability when it came to selling a house. Today, however, a well-constructed and nicely landscaped pool is the opposite. Because of easier cleanup and automated maintenance systems, as well as more tasteful construction that ties a pool to the landscape, pools are often seen as an asset.

While there may be no difference between an in-ground pool and an above-ground pool regarding enjoyment value, there is usually a very real difference when it comes to property value. A well-designed in-ground pool is a permanent structure, adding greatly to the assessed value of your home as well as to its appeal for most future buyers. As a result, you can expect your taxes to rise proportionately after a visit from the tax assessor. An above-ground pool can sometimes be exempted from these taxes, since it is considered a temporary structure. But it is also not likely to add much value to your home and may even detract from its value if you should sell. Before you build, it's a good idea to check with neighbors who have a pool to learn their experiences in your community.

choosing a pool
LOCATION

The variety of stock models available, as well as the ability to create a free-form pool for the same price as a rectangular one, means that there is a pool for nearly every lot.

TIP

SAFETY
▷ For obvious safety reasons, swimming pools and spas can't be located beneath overhead power lines. If need be, the power lines can be moved or buried underground—though doing either will add to the cost of the project.

THINKING ABOUT LOGISTICS

Pay attention to privacy when you think about where to locate your pool. Placing the pool along the street or right next to the neighbor's yard may not make the most sense—although any area can be screened with clever use of plantings and fencing. Also consider the position of the pool with respect to your house. Even if you intend to build a pool house for changing, easy access to your home is a plus. A pool far from the house, or near an inconvenient entrance, such as the front door, can complicate matters.

Another point to consider is access for large construction equipment. While this is not a factor in planning an above-ground pool or portable spa, it becomes essential in helping to determine the location of an in-ground pool. The equipment can't pass over certain obstructions, such as septic tanks, and in general demands a 10-foot-wide access route equivalent to a driveway. In cases where the rear of a lot is inaccessible, it may even require careful

When you're considering where to place a pool, think about how you'll see it from inside the house. The owners of this pool can open their floor-to-ceiling glass doors and enjoy the water view while they eat.

negotiations to obtain a construction right-of-way through a neighbor's yard.

PLACING A POOL ON A STANDARD LOT

Just because a lot is a conventional shape, such as a rectangle, doesn't mean that the pool you build has to be, although it certainly can be.

PLACING A POOL ON AN ODDLY SHAPED LOT

Since an in-ground pool can be constructed in any shape, an oddly shaped lot can actually lead to the creation of a unique and beautiful pool.

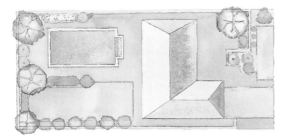

RECTANGULAR POOL
A rectangular pool and a spacious sheltered lawn form two separate backyard recreation areas.

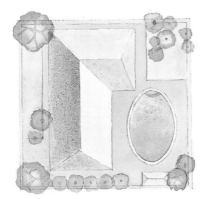

SQUARE LOT
An elliptical pool softens this lot's severe geometry and serves as an elegant focal point in the backyard.

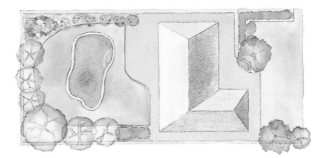

NATURALISTIC POOL
Ringed by a glade of trees, a naturalistic pool creates a forest setting in a small garden.

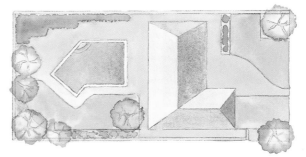

ANGULAR POOL
With the adjacent lawn echoing its contours, this angular pool produces a strikingly contemporary environment in a conventional backyard.

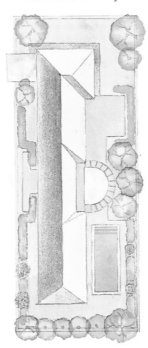

SHALLOW LOT
Creating a number of focal points across the width deepens an extremely shallow lot. This one has a central rounded patio ringed with trees, a rectangular pool and spa on one side, and an entertainment terrace on the other.

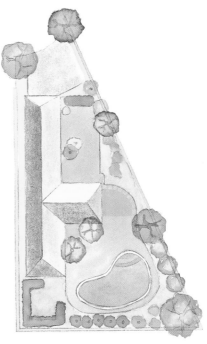

WEDGE-SHAPED LOT
Irregular outdoor spaces lend themselves to distinct activity zones. The generous pool area in one corner provides space for a multitude of pool-related activities. A smaller patio area near the front is private and intimate.

39

choosing a spa
LOCATION

Spas generally offer far more versatility than swimming pools in terms of where they can be located. Although an integral spa has to be adjacent to a swimming pool, portable spas can be positioned anywhere, even indoors.

INSTALLING A SPA INDOORS

Because of the need for privacy and a desire to use the spa year-round, many people opt to have their spa indoors. Here, there are several concerns to address, the first of which are the size and weight of the water-filled unit. To be certain the floor is strong enough to support the thousands of pounds of additional weight, you may need to consult a contractor or structural engineer. In addition, the size of the spa has to be considered because of the difficulty in maneuvering the unit up stairs and through doorways. Although it may be portable, it is hardly small. Finally, think about the best location in the house. Spas, like bathtubs, can create a watery mess around them. Make sure your spa will be in a room that can be cleaned easily and that can withstand trails of water.

An indoor spa might be preferable in colder climates, especially if you will use it for therapeutic reasons. This enclosed patio is an ideal spot. Large windows let the sunlight in, and the tile floor makes splashes easy to clean up.

INSTALLING A SPA OUTDOORS

Although a spa can be located just about anywhere outdoors, it makes sense to install it next to a swimming pool. It's often desirable to provide more privacy for the spa, however, in the form of fencing or screening, and it may also be necessary to shelter the spa to protect it from winter chill.

A spa needs a flat surface that can support its own weight and the weight of the water, which can add thousands of pounds. Placing it on a deck may be an option, but the deck has to be properly constructed in order to handle the load. Ask a contractor or structural engineer if you are unsure. Portable spas can't be placed directly on the ground, as their sheer weight will cause them to settle unevenly over time. Many manufacturers require their spas to be installed on a 4-inch concrete platform, which can be placed or poured on the ground. Despite their name, portable spas cannot be moved easily once installed.

ABOVE: The lower level of a two-tiered garden is an ideal place for an in-ground spa because you'll be able to enjoy more privacy.

BELOW: This spa is tucked around the corner from the house, which is handy if you plan to soak late at night and don't want your voices to wake anyone.

a look at the
WEATHER

Regardless of your climate, giving some thought to sun and wind can result in a pool or spa that is more comfortable in warm weather and can help extend the swimming season in colder climates.

FACTORING IN THE SUN

In most situations, the ideal swimming pool or spa location has a southwest exposure that allows the maximum amount of sunlight at all hours. Although the pool will likely be shadowed in the morning, this probably won't bother early-rising swimmers, who are usually hardy souls. But be sure to take into account your particular climate, since a southwest exposure may not be optimal for your circumstances.

In desert areas where overheating is an issue, a pool facing east or even north will provide some relief from the intense sun. In addition, plantings that shade all or a portion of the pool can help to make things bearable. In northern areas that are comparatively cool in the summertime, a full southern exposure can provide you with more hours of enjoyment in the pool and reduce the cost of heating the water.

TAMING THE WIND

Wind can greatly affect the perceived warmth of a pool or spa as it ripples across the water—and is nearly as important a consideration as sunshine. Too much wind blowing across the area can be unpleasantly chilly, and too little may create a stagnant space on a sweltering day. The ideal is to strike a balance: having a gentle breeze without steady winds or a stifling atmosphere.

Winds vary from region to region, and even from property to property. Some areas of the country are subject to prevailing winds that blow constantly

ABOVE: When temperatures are high, the shade of mature trees and willowy bamboo provides welcome relief.

BELOW: Solid cinder-block walls protect swimmers from wind. In this backyard, the wall is also a backdrop for a raised bed of prickly pear cactus planted behind a mustard yellow wall. A water feature cascades into the pool.

for weeks. Other areas experience daily breezes at particular times of the day. One way to determine the situation in your area is to set up small flags and watch how they move over time, recording your observations. This will help you place the pool or spa for maximum advantage. Fences can also divert and soften the force of breezes (see page 152).

TRACKING THE SUN

AN UNDERSTANDING OF THE DAILY and seasonal patterns of sunlight and shade created on your property will help you place your pool to make maximum use of the available sunlight during swimming hours. Observe and record the movement and effects of the sun's light. And remember that the high summer sun tends to create short shadows and that the lower sun of spring, winter, and fall casts longer shadows, which can affect the pool.

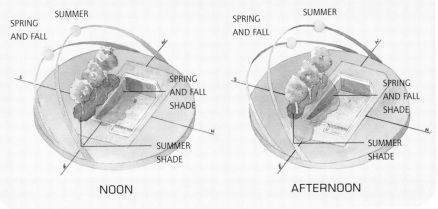

SPRING AND FALL SUMMER

SPRING AND FALL SHADE

SUMMER SHADE

NOON

SPRING AND FALL SUMMER

SPRING AND FALL SHADE

SUMMER SHADE

AFTERNOON

the lay of the
LAND

Two more factors that require careful attention in the construction of a pool or spa are soil and slope. While neither one will likely be extreme enough to eliminate the possibility of building a pool, both can influence your design choices as well as the overall cost of the project.

UNDERSTANDING SOIL TYPE

Once you've chosen the site for your pool, you may need to have a core sample of the land drilled and analyzed by an expert. An experienced pool contractor will be familiar with this process and can either make the analysis or enlist the help of a soils engineer.

GARDEN LOAM   The is the ideal soil. It's easy to dig and drains well.

SANDY SOIL   This type of soil is composed of large particles and is easy to excavate. But the walls of the hole tend to collapse during the process. Excavators may need to prop up the sides of the hole with wooden supports or else spray the walls with concrete to hold them in place as the job proceeds.

CLAY SOIL   This too can be problematic. Consisting of very small, tightly packed particles, clay soil expands when wet, putting tremendous pressure on the finished shell of the pool. This may require extra strengthening with steel or counteracting the force with additional concrete.

BEDROCK   Contractors may need to resort to dynamite to blast the hole for the pool, which can greatly increase construction costs.

A MATTER OF DRAINAGE

Whatever the texture of the soil, if it remains wet because of groundwater, excavation will be difficult; as soon as the hole is dug, it will fill up with water. A remedy for this is a drainage system, and possibly even a sump pump that will remove water as excavation continues. However, both can add hugely to costs. Depending on the severity of the wetness, the drainage system may have to be left in place permanently to prevent groundwater from undermining the pool.

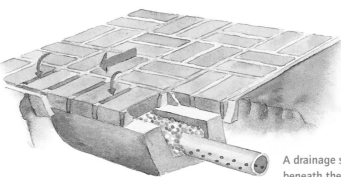

A drainage system beneath the surrounding decking captures rainwater and diverts it from the pool.

WORKING WITH A SLOPE

Few yards are perfectly level, and, in fact, some of the most spectacular pool settings are those built into steep hillsides or even cliffs, with the pool held in place by concrete and steel piers or suspended and cantilevered from below. When designed well, such pools can be magnificent.

Building a pool into a hillside requires special preparation because the pool needs to be engineered and constructed to withstand the pressure of the earth piled on one side and to support the freestanding section on the other side. On the downward-slope side, the pool needs to have a solid foundation similar to the concrete footings that strengthen and support a typical house foundation. In areas where there is bedrock beneath the soil surface, the pool structure can literally be connected to it with giant steel pins. However, retaining walls may be needed on the upward slope to prevent erosion, which would weaken the structure. Such walls may also be needed to resist tremors in areas that are prone to earthquakes. In all cases, a retaining wall higher than 3 feet should be engineered by a professional and may require special permits.

Though steep slopes are generally harder to build on, they can create spectacular settings for a pool or spa. Here, the pool forms a seamless connection with the landscape beyond.

In addition, the area around the pool should be sloped so that rainwater runs away from the pool or spa. Sometimes, drainage pipes are laid beneath the pool decking on top of a gravel bed; gravity then draws the water away from the area (see illustration above). Depending on where the pipe leads, it may be necessary to add a sump pump to remove the accumulating water. Building either system correctly—whether for draining groundwater or for draining rainwater—requires a skilled contractor.

TIP

COST

Even if your particular soil or slope conditions aren't ideal, a swimming pool can almost surely be built on your site. Before proceeding, you should ask the contractor how much extra it will cost to build a pool under the particular conditions. In some cases, the additional work needed to compensate for the slope or the soil type can exceed the actual cost of the pool.

plans and PERMITS

Professional designers and pool contractors can select a site for your pool based on a survey of your yard. However, the more information you have and the more opinions you can present to them, the smoother the process will be.

DRAWING A PRELIMINARY PLOT PLAN

On your own, begin by making a plot plan of your property, an overhead view drawn to scale. You can use low-cost computer software to make elaborate 3-D representations, or you can make a simple scale drawing of your property on graph paper with the location of your house sketched in. If your house and land have already been surveyed, as most have, you can use the survey map for this process; often it's attached to your deed.

Mark the location of your house, along with other features to consider, such as driveways, garages, and any outbuildings, as well as septic fields and septic tanks. Think of the sun exposure, the wind, soil conditions, and any slopes, and mark them on the map in terms of whether they are favorable or unfavorable.

Then you can use tracing paper to experiment with different swimming pool shapes and locations (see illustration, opposite page). This approach allows you to work through various sketches without having to redraw the base plan as you change your ideas. When you meet with a designer or pool

A long, narrow lap pool fits perfectly between this modern house and a bamboo privacy wall.

contractor, arrive with pictures from books and magazines and a clear description of how you intend to use the pool or spa. The more preliminary work you do, the better off you will be.

ZONING AND PERMITS

While above-ground pools and portable spas may qualify as "nonpermanent" structures that don't require local permits, large in-ground swimming pools surely do. In some municipalities, zoning ordinances govern the size and location of pools, including such things as the minimum distance to the nearest property line, as well as the required height of a safety fence. These factors can affect the placement of a swimming pool, so it is best to check in advance with your local building department. In addition, homeowner associations or restrictive covenants in your property deed may further control the possible location of a pool, and it's advisable to investigate these before making plans that will have to be changed.

If it turns out that zoning laws prohibit a pool design or location that you've selected, you may be able to file for a variance. Keep in mind, though, that this can be a lengthy and uncertain process, and it usually requires obtaining the consent of your neighbors. Contractors typically will take care of the filing for whatever permits are necessary, but a request for a variance requires the homeowner's participation.

TIP

SMART

When considering the location for an outdoor pool or spa, pay attention to how it will look from inside the house. You may want it to become a focal point to be seen from certain windows, or you may prefer to conceal it from view, especially if it will be closed off during the winter.

After sketching your lot and your house to scale on graph paper, you can experiment with several different pool locations. Take a look at access, as well as weather factors.

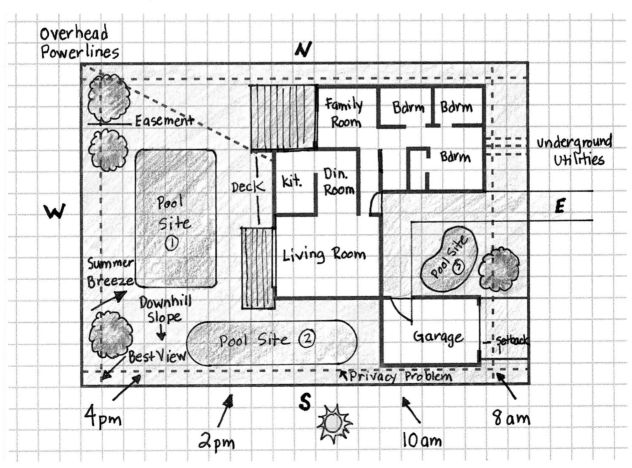

finding pool
PROFESSIONALS

Once you have your basic ideas and pool possibilities firmly in mind, it will be easy to work effectively with professionals. These can include architects or designers as well as contractors. Some companies offer both design and construction services.

Because you'll have to be able to work with someone for the duration of the project—which can be many months in some cases—this is as much a search for compatible personalities as it is for expert skills and reasonable costs.

CHECKING REFERENCES

No matter how you find a contractor to interview—through an ad, a sign in front of a project, a referral from a neighbor—it's essential to check references. Ask to see a portfolio of the person's work stretching back five years or longer, and request the names of all clients during that period. Reputable professionals will willingly give you this information. Then call several clients and ask how the project went. When you find projects similar to yours in scope and size, arrange to see them so you can judge for yourself the quality of the work. Most homeowners welcome the opportunity to help someone along.

WHAT TO ASK CONTRACTORS

• May I have a list of references that extends back for the past five years?

• Are all workers insured for workers' compensation and general liability?

• Have you worked on any projects that are similar in scope and cost to the one that I'm planning to build?

• How will cost overruns be managed? Will there be an agreed-upon price— or a pay-as-you-go arrangement?

• Who will be doing the work—the contractor or a team of subcontractors?

WHAT TO ASK FELLOW HOMEOWNERS

• Did the contractor perform the work as expected?

• Was the project completed within budget?

• Did the contractor work steadily, or were there unexplained gaps in the process?

• If there were cost overruns, were they properly explained?

• Did the contractor return promptly to make any follow-up repairs?

• If you were to do the project over again, would you use the same contractor?

SOLICITING BIDS

Ideally, several contractors will be competing for your project, but this requires that the work be spelled out in detail—including exact sizes, specific materials, and the brand names of equipment. Otherwise, estimates could vary widely because one contractor may include something that another assumed would be supplied by someone else. If you have a single contractor in mind and don't plan to get competing bids, check with neighbors, friends, and the contractor's past clients to see what they paid for similar projects.

WORKING WITH A DESIGNER

While most pool contractors can also design a standard pool, you may want something more distinctive. It might be a swimming pool with an unusual shape, a series of terraces that connect the pool with your home, or a pool house that reflects the style of your residence. Some contractors can handle these challenges alone, but in many cases a separate architect or designer will have to be brought in to help tie everything together.

Such creativity comes at a cost. Some architects and designers charge a flat fee based on the scope of the project; others charge an hourly rate, which can range anywhere from $50 to $100. Some provide construction-management services and take a percentage of the total cost as their fee.

Because of the myriad choices and the engineering challenges that go into creating an elaborate pool and setting such as this one, the assistance of an architect or a professional designer is essential.

SIGNING THE CONTRACT

Be sure to get estimates in writing rather than over the phone. Set a reasonable dead-line—a week, perhaps—to make your deci-sion, especially if you're waiting for other bids. Don't bow to pressure from a con-tractor to make up your mind quickly.

The contractor best suited for the job may not necessarily be the person who gave you the lowest bid. In fact, it may be the one who submitted the highest bid but whom you prefer based on personality, quality of work, and references. If the contractor you prefer gave you a high estimate, it may be possible to negotiate the fee downward by showing that person the other estimates.

Once you make your choice, be sure that the contract spells out an expected start date, a completion date, and a schedule of pay-ments. The contract should also specify that the contractor and all subcontractors agree to provide certificates of general liability

Building a large in-ground swimming pool is a major construction project. Because of the high costs and liabilities involved, it's impor-tant to protect yourself by choosing a contrac-tor wisely and carefully reviewing the contract.

insurance and workers' compensation insur-ance for all employees on the job.

A contract is a legally binding document. Before signing it, consider having your attorney review it to spare you any future difficulties.

In some cases, contractors insist on receiving a deposit when the contract is signed. This should be no more than a token amount, and it is limited in some states to $200. To protect yourself, pay for work only as it is completed, rather than up front. The final payment should be made only after the building inspector has signed off on all the work and the project is com-pleted to your satisfaction.

INSURING SUCCESS

While homeowners tend to focus on the credibility of a contractor and his or her price, another very important aspect to consider is insurance. The fact is that anyone hurt while working at your home can sue you for medical bills, lost wages, and more, unless the contractor who hires the person is adequately insured.

Ask for certificates showing proof of insurance. You should expect to see liability coverage of at least $1 million per occurrence. Request to be listed as additionally insured on your contractor's policy so that your name will appear right on the insurance certificate. Contractors should also have workers' compensation insurance for all their employees, as well as an umbrella policy that extends to subcontractors.

UNDERSTANDING LIEN WAIVERS

For a project as complicated as constructing a swimming pool, a single contractor will probably not be able to do it all. Independent subcontractors may perform work such as excavating the site, building decks, adding the landscaping, and installing electrical equipment.

While subcontractors are paid directly by the contractor, you should protect yourself by making sure that all the subcontractors are in fact paid for their work. Otherwise, they may try to collect any outstanding fees from you. Ask the contractor to supply a signed lien waiver from each subcontractor, which certifies that the subcontractor has been paid in full for any work completed.

PLANNING A SCHEDULE

ALTHOUGH THERE IS NO standard schedule for building a pool, the following rough time line can help you understand the process. The steps noted here should take place before construction begins.

12 MONTHS BEFORE THE START
Begin researching what you'd like to build by looking at magazines, other homes, and showrooms. Start creating an idea file as well as a wish list, making one column for things you must have and a separate one for things you would like.

10 TO 12 MONTHS AHEAD
Begin figuring out a budget for the pool, and consider payment possibilities—including a home equity line of credit or other loan. Also, begin asking relatives and friends to recommend designers and contractors.

6 TO 8 MONTHS AHEAD
Interview contractors and designers. Take them your idea file and wish list.

2 TO 6 MONTHS AHEAD
Refine your plan to a detailed spec sheet. Solicit competitive bids or negotiate with one selected contractor if you have a preference. After choosing the contractor, decide on start and finish dates, then have an attorney look over the contract before you sign it.

DESIGN

THE MORE YOU UNDERSTAND about the possible materials and design choices, the better you'll be able to create a pool or spa that meets your needs at a price you can afford. Keep in mind that because contractors tend to specialize in a particular type of pool or spa, your choice of contractor will influence the overall design.

in-ground
POOLS

In-ground pools offer the most flexibility in terms of size and style, ranging from traditional shapes to free-form fantasies. Not only can these pools be fitted into irregular lots or specific areas in your yard, but they can be designed to mirror the style of your house.

A MATTER OF SIZE

Barring any special needs, such as a training pool for competitive swimmers or a pool large enough to handle a weekly water polo match, a backyard pool can usually be fairly small. The standard pool dimensions—20 by 40 feet, or even 15 by 30 feet—provide 450 to 800 square feet of swimming area, enough for serious exercise or aquatic fun.

In fact, a new trend is toward pools that are smaller than 400 square feet, which can fulfill most families' demands. The advantages of smaller pools are that they can fit into the landscape more easily, they cost less to construct, and they require less money to maintain. Such "boutique pools" also have an element of intimacy that's more difficult to achieve with larger pools.

POOL SHAPES

Even with a modest-size pool, there are an enormous number of shape choices besides rectangles and the classic kidney design. As a rule, though, reasonably simple is best. Shapes based on rectangles, circles, and ovals won't overwhelm the landscaping. Nor will

they require complicated decking or sophisticated planting schemes around them. In certain cases, though, oddly shaped pools may make the most sense—such as when you have a small, awkwardly shaped lot or want to preserve a large tree, rock outcropping, or other landscape feature.

ABOVE: A large pool can fill up an entire yard and provide a spectacular centerpiece for entertaining.

LEFT: Take cues from the landscape to develop a natural shape for your pool.

TIP

DESIGN One way to narrow the seemingly limitless possibilities for the shape of an in-ground pool is to select one that best complements the style of your house, whether traditional or contemporary, formal or casual.

ADDING WATER FEATURES

A waterfall that spills from an in-ground spa into a pool provides a soothing and visually appealing connection between the two. Rather than extravagant, such a water feature can be relatively inexpensive if it's built when the pool is, since it will use the same pump and circulation system. The construction—which involves elevating the spa several inches above the pool so that the water spills by gravity—is simple to engineer. However, adding a spa with a waterfall after the pool is completed can be difficult and expensive.

Likewise, it's relatively inexpensive to integrate a fountain into the pool's pump and filtration systems during pool construction. Adding a fountain later, though, requires draining the pool, drilling through the side, and installing new plumbing. While this can be practical if it is part of an extensive overhaul of the pool, it wouldn't be a cost-effective project on its own.

ABOVE: A waterfall or fountain can be a mesmerizing addition to a pool. This example is perhaps more dramatic than most, as water pours off high groupings of boulders to create the feeling of a tropical paradise.

LEFT: Spiky plants atop stone columns frame this two-tiered waterfall, creating a striking architectural look.

OPPOSITE PAGE: Arching streams of water provide a pleasant sound when the pool is not in use.

ACCESS FOR ALL

GIVEN THE THERAPEUTIC BENEFITS of swimming, an at-home pool makes a wonderful addition for people with physical disabilities or limitations. There are several ways the physically challenged can maneuver easily and safely in and out of the water, either alone or with assistance.

With an in-ground pool, the most user-friendly solution is a ramp that leads directly from the surrounding decking into the water. It can be built at the same time as the pool, in lieu of steps. Paired with a handrail that extends up and onto the deck, such a ramp works well for people who can't navigate steps easily, and also provides access for those using an aquatic wheelchair.

Devices that can be added to an existing in-ground pool include a specially designed pool ladder with broader, closely spaced steps, and a portable ramp that extends from the deck into the water. If you're considering such a device, look for pool contractors who have experience installing them or who specialize in the design of pools for people with physical disabilities. They'll know which options are best for your circumstances.

For an above-ground pool, where a ramp isn't feasible, a comparatively low-cost option is an electronic lift, which hoists a seated person from the ground up and into the pool.

choosing
MATERIALS

An in-ground pool starts with a hole similar to the kind dug for a house foundation. The hole can be lined with either concrete, vinyl, or fiberglass, which vary in cost and durability.

CONCRETE

Of all the materials available for pool construction, concrete with a plaster finish is by far the most durable. In addition to providing sheer stability, the surface is easy to replaster, resulting in a pool that has a long life span.

In years past, builders created concrete pools by erecting wooden forms, then pouring wet concrete into the molds, much as a house foundation is constructed. But the advent of spray-on concrete—either shotcrete or gunite—has drastically reduced the cost of construction and allowed tremendous flexibility in design.

Once the hole is excavated, the sides and the bottom are lined with steel rods called rebar, which greatly increases the strength of the pool's walls and provides the elasticity needed to resist cracks. The rebar can be positioned to create nearly any shape conceivable, as well as customized steps or ramps.

ABOVE: Beyond durability, concrete provides flexibility in design. It's a great choice when space is limited and when you need an unusual shape or size.

LEFT: You can use any type of coping, edging, and deck material with a concrete pool. If you stick with concrete coping, consider adding a decorative finish or color.

Then either shotcrete or gunite is sprayed on. The two materials are very similar; the difference lies in the way they are mixed. Shotcrete is delivered to the site already mixed and is then mixed further with air and sprayed onto the rebar with a hose. Gunite is delivered dry, then mixed with water and air as it is sprayed into place. Because it can be mixed at the site as it's needed, gunite is more popular than shotcrete, but they produce identical linings when applied correctly.

Not only does this spray-on technology give a contractor absolute freedom in determining the size and shape of a concrete swimming pool, but in most cases the price is based on the pool's perimeter. That means that a pool with contemporary curves will cost no more than the same size pool with right angles.

Even though they're prefabricated, vinyl pools are available in a range of shapes and sizes. A vinyl pool is much quicker to install than one made of concrete.

VINYL

The advent of vinyl for lining in-ground pools has produced a surge in construction because of both the lower cost (see page 35) and the easier installation compared with shotcrete or gunite. Instead of requiring a month or more, building a vinyl-lined pool usually can be completed in a matter of days.

Vinyl pools are actually a combination of a large, flexible container—the liner—and supporting walls made of aluminum, steel, plastic, masonry block, or even wood. The bottom of the liner rests on a bed of flattened sand or other material, while its top is secured by material called coping that creates a finished edge to the pool and serves as a border for the deck. Vinyl-lined pools are manufactured in dozens of different styles, sizes, and colors, so although customizing isn't possible, most homeowners will find a good fit.

Vinyl deteriorates over time as a result of exposure to ultraviolet radiation and to pool chemicals. Typically, a vinyl liner will last 10 to 12 years. To prevent fading and staining, some liners include ultraviolet and fungus inhibitors, which extend the life of the liner to 18 or 20 years. In many cases, replacing the liner is a straightforward matter—although doing so will most likely cost between $5,000 and $10,000. But if the pool is built in clay soil, which expands when wet, the liner can't be replaced easily. If this is your situation, you'll have to excavate again and completely rebuild the pool.

FIBERGLASS

For ease of in-ground pool construction, nothing can match fiberglass. Be aware, though, that it may be more expensive than concrete and is not as long-lasting.

A fiberglass swimming pool is sold as a gigantic one-piece shell that is delivered to your home by truck and set in place in an excavated hole with the use of a crane. Then the plumbing and electrical systems are connected to the outside wall.

Because fiberglass pools are purchased ready-made, it is not possible to request

COMPARISON OF MATERIALS

TYPE	COST	EASE OF PROJECT	LONGEVITY
Concrete (shotcrete or gunite)	high	complex	excellent
Fiberglass	high	simple	good
Vinyl	low	moderate	good

a customized design—but most manufacturers offer dozens of models and sizes to choose from, complete with preformed steps, spas, and benches.

In years past, the quality of fiberglass pools was inferior to the alternatives, leading to problems such as leaks and buckling. Advances in technology have largely eliminated these weaknesses. But the sheer size of such pools limits their availability, as it is expensive to truck them over great distances.

The basic form of a fiberglass pool is made on an upside-down mold. Then a coating is applied to create a smooth inside surface. This slick surface is difficult for algae to cling to, making it easy to keep a fiberglass pool clean. But over 10 to 15 years, the combined forces of sunlight and pool chemicals begin to deteriorate the surface and turn it slightly chalky. Recoating it is tricky because the new coating does not adhere easily to the old. Recoating a fiberglass pool also requires that it be completely drained, but since the pool itself does not offer much structural support, draining may cause cave-ins if the pool has been constructed in an expansive soil such as clay.

NATURAL POOLS

IF YOU WOULD PREFER A POOL that looks more like a swimming hole found in nature, or if you are sensitive to chemicals, consider building a natural pool. They are seen more often in Europe but are gaining popularity in the United States. Natural swimming pools rely on plants to create a self-cleaning ecosystem so that chlorine and other chemicals are not needed. The pools can be constructed of gravel stone and clay instead of concrete for a rustic look, or you can add plants to an existing pool, as was done above.

A natural pool is divided into swimming and plant areas. The plants add oxygen to the water and support bacteria that eat debris and other organisms. Water moves back and forth from the swimming area to the plant area for filtering via PVC pipes. The water also needs to be aerated regularly so it does not become stagnant. Waterfalls are one way to do it, but underwater aeration systems are more effective.

Search for a builder who has experience constructing natural swimming pools, as there is a science to them.

A fiberglass pool—even an extremely large one—arrives at the site ready-made and is then carefully positioned in the excavated hole.

above-ground
POOLS

While not as luxurious as in-grounds, above-ground pools have their distinct advantages. They are inexpensive and easy to install. Because they are classified as non-permanent structures, adding one does not usually require a building permit and will not increase your real estate taxes.

A POOL ON THE GO

If you envision a pool as a permanent addition to your home, an in-ground pool makes the best sense from an investment perspective. But an above-ground pool can be disassembled and transported in a moving van, making it a popular choice for renters or for those who are planning a move sometime soon. It's also a good option if you want a pool just for a few years while your children are young.

POOLS IN AN INSTANT

All of the hassles of constructing an in-ground pool—from getting building permits to having major earth-moving equipment rumbling through the backyard—vanish with above-ground models. Above-ground pools require little or no excavation, cost a fraction of the price of an in-ground pool, and can be installed by a savvy do-it-yourself homeowner, which will further reduce costs. It's no wonder that more above-ground pools are sold each year than in-ground ones.

For all its ease, though, a portable pool can be difficult to assemble correctly.

Unless it's small or extremely simple, installing it will most likely require the help of a swimming pool dealer (see more about installation on pages 124–127).

MATERIALS

Above-ground pools tend to have more uniformity than the great variety of materials, styles, and construction techniques available for in-ground pools. In general,

these pools sit directly on the ground and require no excavation other than simple grading to create a flat surface. Most have a constant depth through-out—usually about 4 feet—although shapes can vary from rectangular to circular. In most cases, above-ground pools contain vinyl liners that are held in place by self-supporting walls made of galvanized steel, plastic, or aluminum.

SITING AN ABOVE-GROUND POOL

These versatile pools can be set up in a wide variety of sites, usually requir-ing only a flat surface and reasonable access. Be sure to follow the same guidelines as for an in-ground pool (see pages 38–39).

With astute planning, an above-ground pool can become an enticing element in a yard. Here, a sloping site makes it possible to build a deck around part of the pool, which gives it a built-in look.

CREATING A PERMANENT LOOK

Above-ground swimming pools benefit greatly from simple additions that make them seem more at home in a yard. This might be fencing that conceals the pool's underpinnings from view, or a basic deck. In many cases, the pool kit itself contains decking, ranging from a small sitting area on one side to a surface that surrounds the entire pool and is wide enough for furniture and entertaining.

If your pool kit doesn't contain decking, it's possible to build a deck separately. This works especially well if you can site the pool on a flat surface a few feet lower than the house. Then the deck can connect from the house directly to the top of the swimming pool, creating the illusion of an in-ground pool.

FINDING A REPUTABLE DEALER

Quality and warranties vary widely for above-ground pools, even more so than for in-ground ones. Advertisements often lure shoppers with offers of low prices, but the chances that you'll end up with an inferior product when shopping by price alone are great. Here's how to ensure that the above-ground pool you choose will last:

• Ask the dealer for the names and telephone numbers of customers from the

RIGHT: Creative landscaping makes an above-ground pool every bit as beautiful as one of its more expensive cousins. A richness of hedges and tiered plantings cleverly conceals this pool's humble design.

BELOW: Here, the focus is on the elaborate decking and plantings, which enhance the overall appeal of the modest pool.

past several years, not just the past season. Call them up and visit as many of the pools as you can in person to make sure the quality is what you expect. The goal is to see how the pools hold up over time, rather than how inviting they look a month after installation.

• Read product reviews of the various pools you are considering, either in consumer magazines or through an Internet search. Often, various models produced by dif-

ferent manufacturers will look identical, but some will be far more durable than others for the same price.

• Make sure you understand the warranty, as well as the dealer's ability to remedy any problems that may arise. Be wary of warranties that cover only parts and materials and not the labor required to install them. In most cases, the charge for parts is very little compared to the cost of having them replaced.

an enclosed
POOL

A pool inside an enclosure offers various advantages over one that's exposed to the elements. You can either construct one indoors or enclose an outdoor pool.

ENCLOSING AN OUTDOOR POOL

Enclosures for pools range in materials and design from simple to luxurious. Geodesic domes are fitted inexpensively over existing pools. They extend the swimming season by trapping heat in the manner of a greenhouse. In most cases, domes are removed during the summer, when they tend to overheat the pool. Another option is a screened enclosure (pictured at right). Popular in warm places like Florida, screened enclosures allow you to swim "outdoors" without worrying about bugs. If you live in an area with harsh winters, you may need removable support posts to hold the structure up under the weight of the snow.

More elaborate enclosures resemble greenhouse conservatories. Permanent structures with glass panels and roofs, they provide a year-round swimming and entertaining environment, complete with heating and cooling systems for maximum comfort. The cost of these enclosures can far exceed the cost of the pool itself

Screened enclosures allow you to enjoy the fresh air while keeping insects away.

because of the mechanical systems that run them and the level of finish work needed to complete them.

For financial reasons, you may decide to build an outdoor pool now and defer adding an enclosure to it until sometime in the future. Be sure to locate mechanical equipment wisely so that it won't interfere with the placement of the enclosure. If the enclosure you're planning requires a foundation, you can save money by building it during the construction of the pool, when the excavation equipment is already on site.

BUILDING A POOL INDOORS

Most often, constructing an indoor pool will involve adding on to your house. It's important to follow the usual guidelines for an addition—consulting an architect, hiring a contractor, and so forth. The pool's location is crucial. You may want to site it near a bathroom or another room with a non-carpeted floor. More important, you'll need to deal with the issues of chemical odors and humidity.

While the odor of a pool throughout the house can simply be annoying, the humidity that builds up can cause serious problems, such as mold and rot. To prevent this, you'll need to build a true separation between the house and the pool, in the form of a corridor or doors that prevent air from transferring.

In addition, the pool area will need adequate ventilation so that the vapors can be transferred outdoors. The ideal ventilation system will depend on the

Swimming in this indoor pool surrounded by windows that let in natural light is almost like swimming outside.

size of the pool, the dimensions of the enclosure, and the average temperature of the pool area. When choosing a contractor, be sure to enlist one who has experience building indoor pools. Also visit several of his or her previous projects to check their conditions, preferably after the pools have been in use for many years.

pool finishes and
TRIM

Vinyl-lined and fiber-glass pools need no additional interior finishes, but concrete pools require a plaster coating for the inside, as well as coping, a covering for the edge of the pool. Both surfaces present the opportunity to add decorative accents that can greatly enhance the pool's appearance.

INTERIOR FINISHES

Despite being watertight, gunite and shotcrete interiors need an additional finish coat to create a smooth surface. The traditional choice is white plaster, which forms a waterproof, durable, nonskid skin that reflects the sky to produce the cool blue that is so characteristic of swimming pools.

In recent years, pool plaster has been mixed with other materials to create aggregates that produce different effects. Adding pulverized marble dust, for instance, increases the plaster's longevity and alters its reflecting properties. If it is white, marble dust yields a slightly deeper blue reflection of the sky. Gray aggregate produces a pool that appears greenish-blue; black creates a very dark yet inviting look that mimics the color of a creek in nature. In all cases, a pool finished with aggregate looks drastically different once it is filled with water compared with when it is empty.

Take your interior finish up a notch by creating a work of art with mosaic tiles.

COPING

Coping serves a practical function: It conceals the concrete edge of the pool and provides a nonskid surface to walk on. But it also can serve as a decorative accent. The coping for a concrete pool can be made from such materials as precast concrete, tile, and natural stones. Beware, however, of using colored precast stones, as the dye in them can leach out over time and filter into the pool.

One alternative to adding a stone coping is enlarging the pool's concrete or wooden decking so that it extends slightly over the edge all the way around. No matter which material you use, though, be careful to install the coping at the correct angle—tilted slightly away from the pool. Coping should direct any splashed water and rainwater away from the pool, helping to keep the pool water clean.

ABOVE: To create the look of a natural swimming hole, the bottom of this vinyl-lined pool is covered with coarse sand. At the edges, blue-gray plaster and stone tiles create a gradual edge without traditional coping. The result is about as close to the feel of swimming in a lagoon as you'll get in an urban backyard.

LEFT: Mosaic tiles and embedded stones turned this coping into a design feature that adds to the overall style of the backyard.

underwater
LIGHTING

If a pool or spa is to be used in the evening, proper lighting is essential for safety. But lighting also creates an opportunity to add interesting accents. Incandescent lighting must be put in during construction, but fiber-optic technology has do-it-yourself possibilities for an existing pool.

INCANDESCENT LIGHTING

Safety considerations may incline you toward incandescent lighting, which provides strong illumination. To eliminate the risk of shock that results from combining electrical connections with water, these lights come completely sealed inside a protective waterproof niche.

But because the bulbs are sealed along with the fixtures, changing them when they burn out requires a little extra effort. You literally pull the light out of the pool wall on its specially designed extension cord, bringing it to the surface, where you replace the burnt-out bulb. You then reposition the entire apparatus in the waterproof niche.

Because of the engineering involved in constructing an underwater lighting system and the difficulty of wiring a pool, these lights need to be installed when the pool is built—they are nearly impossible to install afterward.

TIP

DESIGN

The services of a lighting designer are often available free of charge when you purchase lighting, so take advantage of a professional's expertise.

FIBER-OPTIC LIGHTING

With this type of lighting, a cord carries light, rather than electricity, to the pool. A lens at the end of the cord releases the illumination, eliminating any electrical hazards. Because the electric source lies outside the pool, fiber-optic lights are ideal for adding to an existing pool. A knowledgeable homeowner can safely and easily do the job without a contractor.

Fiber-optic lighting tends to be far more subtle than the incandescent variety, creating many aesthetic possibilities for accent lighting, both within the pool and just beneath the coping that encircles it. Resist the temptation to add too many fiber-optic lights; the result can be a chaotic nighttime scene. Add lights sparingly to create a simple effect rather than a dazzling light show.

ABOVE: When properly conceived, lighting is as much a part of the pool landscape as decking and plantings.

RIGHT: Include the pool in your overall backyard lighting plan. Here, incandescent pool lighting creates a soft blue glow that complements a nearby tree illuminated by two spotlights.

OPPOSITE PAGE: In a house with so many windows, underwater lighting allows the homeowners to enjoy the landscape even after the sun goes down.

understanding
SPAS

The term "spa" refers to any small pool that contains benches for seating, jets, and a heater. Integral spas are connected directly to swimming pools. Portable spas can be set up anywhere indoors or out, while traditional hot tubs can be made of wood and may or may not have churning action.

IN-GROUND SPAS

For people who already have a swimming pool or are building one, the easiest way to create a spa is to build one right into the pool. The spa can be made of the same materials as the pool and connected to the same water supply and filtration systems. You can also save considerably on heating costs, since the water may already be heated in the pool. Even if the swimming pool is closed off for the winter, it is possible to use the spa portion year-round, although you may need to take extra steps to protect plumbing systems from freezing (see page 215).

People without a swimming pool can build a spa directly into the ground in the manner of a miniature swimming pool, which is how spas were originally built. However, the expense of this sort of construction has made this choice unpopular. Because of the extensive plumbing and electrical systems involved, a stand-alone in-ground spa can cost nearly two-thirds the amount of a full-sized swimming pool.

OPPOSITE PAGE: A pergola offers some sun protection and provides a spot to mount outdoor speakers so you can enjoy music while soaking.

BELOW: In an indoor-outdoor space, you get the best of both worlds: fresh air but also protection from the elements. It's the perfect spot for an in-ground spa.

RIGHT: An integrated spa like this one can be built at the same time as the pool, or years later.

CLASSIC HOT TUBS

Usually made of wood such as rot-resistant redwood or red cedar, these spas are built like giant barrels, with staves of wood held together by steel hoops. As the staves swell with water, they form a leakproof seal and a perfect—and picturesque—tub. Classic hot tubs can be fitted with jets to create whirlpool action, or left as still pools with just the action of the filter to keep the water moving.

These wooden tubs have suffered in reputation in recent years, mostly because wood is not as sanitary as other surfaces. But they can be fitted with a vinyl liner, which eliminates the hygiene problem. Paying careful attention to the water filtration and chemistry will also keep a classic tub fresh and viable (see pages 192–201).

ABOVE: This portable spa has a more permanent look surrounded by a flagstone wall and edging.

OPPOSITE PAGE TOP: Wooden hot tubs have a rustic beauty all their own.

OPPOSITE PAGE BOTTOM: Choosing a prefabricated spa for a vacation house is more cost-effective than installing an in-ground spa.

PORTABLE SPAS

A newer addition to the world of spas and hot tubs is the portable spa. The plumbing and electrical systems come completely assembled in these units, and the filtration system is self-contained, which makes them easy to set up either indoors or out. They generally require no building permit and will not raise property taxes, as they are not permanent structures. Sizes vary widely, from small 125-gallon versions that seat two to larger 500-gallon styles that seat eight.

Some portable spas run on standard 120 volts, so they can be plugged into any receptacle. Others run on 240 volts, similar to electric dryers. Although the latter need to be connected by an electrician, they have greater heating capacity, and the jets can be used in combination with heaters.

CHOOSING THE RIGHT SPA

Spas come in a huge variety of both styles and quality. The market is saturated with cheap portable spas that may not hold up. To make sure you choose a spa that lasts, avoid impulse shopping. Research the specific brands you're considering by looking up product reviews on the Internet, asking friends and relatives for their recommendations, and spending time at spa dealers testing out their various models. Large dealers have working display models in their showrooms that you can try on the spot, so be sure to take your bathing suit.

A SPA TO SWIM IN

A SWIM SPA combines the compact size of a spa with the exercise possibilities of a pool. Most swim spas are 13 to 15 feet long and 6 to 8 feet wide—far smaller than a swimming pool yet easily twice the length of a standard spa.

Strong jets create a swirling current to swim against, allowing you to get a workout by swimming in place. The water is usually kept cooler than in a spa, since exercising in warm water can be exhausting, but the temperature can easily be raised for a hotter soak. In some models, a removable partition makes it possible to heat a small portion of the spa for soaking, while leaving the remainder at a lower temperature for swimming.

One word of warning: Not all swimmers enjoy using a swim spa, which is the aquatic equivalent of running on a treadmill. Before purchasing one, be sure to try it out at a dealer's showroom.

EQUIPMENT

WHAT'S THE MOST APPEALING FEATURE of a pool or spa? For most people, it's clear, sparkling water at the perfect temperature. Achieving this inviting state depends in part on managing the water chemistry (discussed on pages 192–201) but the pool or spa's mechanical equipment plays a big role as well. Understanding that system—which circulates, filters, and warms the water—will help you make efficient, cost-effective choices.

water
WORKS

Water in a swimming pool needs to circulate in order to stay fresh. Circulation helps mix chemicals in the water and dilute heated water evenly to prevent warm spots and cold spots. Most important, it makes it possible to strain and filter out any debris or particulates in the water.

SWIMMING POOL PIPES AND PLUMBING

Just behind the walls and underneath the deck of an in-ground swimming pool—or attached to the outside wall of an above-ground pool—lies a network of pipes that rivals a home's plumbing system in complexity.

The water within a pool's support system flows under pressure in a continuous loop. Water drains from the pool, either through the main drain or through side drains called skimmers. Next it passes through a pump that pressurizes it, forcing it through a filter and a heater (if the pool has one). From there, the water travels through return lines and sprays back into the pool through nozzles known as inlets.

ABOVE: A pool's plumbing system is the essential element in keeping water clean.

LEFT: A complicated network of plumbing keeps the water circulating in a pool or spa so that it can be filtered and heated.

TIP

C O S T

In a house, the best pipes for delivering water are made of copper. Not so in a pool. Because this water is not for drinking, plastic pipes made from PVC or the similar CPVC are perfectly safe and offer several advantages. They're inexpensive, easy to work with, and—most important—resistant to corrosion.

BEHIND THE SCENES OF A SWIMMING POOL

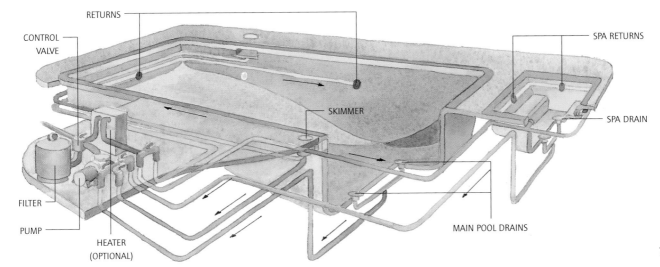

RETURNS

CONTROL VALVE

SPA RETURNS

SKIMMER

SPA DRAIN

FILTER

PUMP

HEATER (OPTIONAL)

MAIN POOL DRAINS

skimmers, drains, and
INLETS

Skimmers and drains draw water into the pump and the filtration system, then inlets return clean water back into the pool. Here's how these devices work together.

SURFACE SKIMMERS

As their name suggests, these devices help keep pools clean by skimming water and capturing any floating debris, such as leaves and grass clippings. Essentially, they do the same job as gutters do in large commercial swimming pools. They're built into the upper sides of an in-ground pool, where their suction action draws in pool litter and traps it. Convenient access permits the

trapped debris to be emptied easily. Skimmers also create an opening for attaching a portable aquatic vacuum. The vacuum's tube connects to the skimmer's suction line and is powered by the pool pump.

A typical surface skimmer is made of precast concrete or plastic and consists of a tank with a projecting throat on its upper side (see the illustration at left). A self-adjusting piece of plastic, called a weir, performs the skimming action by regulating the amount of water that enters the skimmer. Because the weir adjusts to allow only a thin layer of water to spill over, water is pulled off the surface rapidly—effectively keeping a large area of the pool surface clear.

In general, one well-located skimmer can keep up to 500 square feet of pool surface clean. However, if the debris that's gathered by a skimmer is left to accumulate, it will put extra strain on the pump. For best results, the skimmer basket should be cleaned out each day.

Skimmers must be installed with an equalizer line—a pipe that connects from the bottom of the skimmer basket through the pool wall and into the water. The equalizer prevents air from

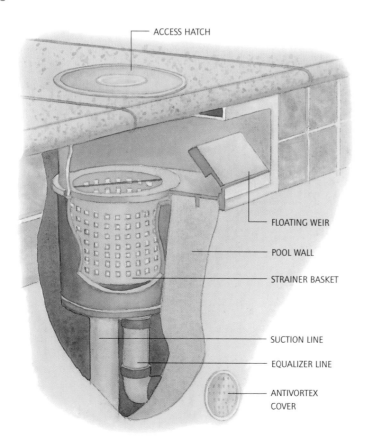

ACCESS HATCH

FLOATING WEIR

POOL WALL

STRAINER BASKET

SUCTION LINE

EQUALIZER LINE

ANTIVORTEX COVER

being sucked into the system if evaporation causes the water level to drop below the level of the weir. If air were to enter the system, it would cause the pump to stall.

ABOVE-GROUND POOL SKIMMERS

Because above-ground pools have thin walls, it is not possible to place skimmer baskets within them. Instead, special collector units that hang on the side of the pool or float in the water can be attached to the pump mechanism to provide effective skimming action (see the illustration below). One drawback, however, is that these units project into the pool instead of lying flush with the wall, creating a swimming obstacle. The hand skimmer is a labor-intensive alternative. It's simply a large net that you pass over the water surface to catch and remove debris. This would need to be done daily to effectively replace a floating skimmer.

Crystal-clear water is the key ingredient of a beautiful pool, as in this pristine in-ground example. To keep the surface free of debris, the strainer baskets should be cleaned regularly.

FLOATING SKIMMER FOR
ABOVE-GROUND POOL

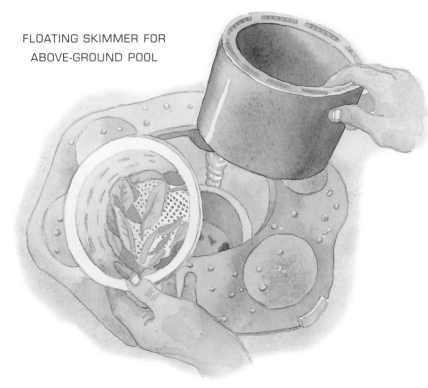

TIP

QUICK

Skimmers are most effective when located on the downwind side of the pool, as wind will push debris toward the opening.

MAIN DRAIN

DRAINS

In addition to skimmers, most pools have a pair of main drains at the bottom, usually situated at the deepest point in the pool, with the entire floor slanting toward them. Debris, which naturally settles to the lowest area, is sucked automatically through the main drains toward the pump, then through the filter.

THE ANTIVORTEX COVER If you've ever placed your hand over the main drain in a swimming pool, you've felt the tug generated by the pump. In pools with two drains and multiple skimmer baskets, having one blocked drain will not create a dangerous situation. But where there is only one drain, a blocked flow can create a hazardous form of suction known as a vortex. This strong pull can trap swimmers even in a shallow pool, posing a grave danger. Having multiple drains and skimmers reduces the risk but doesn't eliminate it.

ANTIVORTEX COVER

To further enhance safety, all drains—as well as all equalizers installed with skimmers—should be fitted with an antivortex cover. This slatted or perforated cover (shown below left), similar to a drain cover in a shower, prevents hair and limbs from becoming caught in the plumbing. If antivortex covers are in place and the pool is built and operated correctly, there is virtually no risk of suction pinning someone against a drain.

HYDROSTATIC VALVE ANATOMY

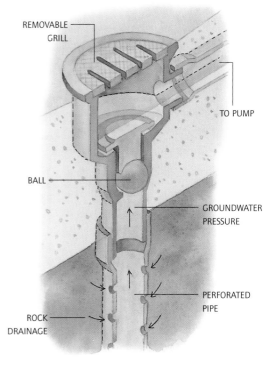

REMOVABLE GRILL

TO PUMP

BALL

GROUNDWATER PRESSURE

PERFORATED PIPE

ROCK DRAINAGE

THE HYDROSTATIC VALVE Groundwater that lies beneath the swimming pool is not a problem as long as the pool is filled; the sheer weight of the water keeps the pool structure firmly in place. If the pool is emptied, however, groundwater exerts tremendous pressure against the bottom and sides of the pool. This pressure can be so great that it cracks concrete pools and causes fiberglass pools to lift up out of the ground.

Fitting each main drain with a hydrostatic relief valve prevents the problem. The valve consists of a floating ball that lies in a pipe between the drain and the groundwater. During normal operation, water in the pool presses down against the ball and seals the drain off from the groundwater. When the pool is empty, however, the ball floats up and unblocks the pipe if the pressure from the groundwater increases to dangerous levels. Then the pool fills with harmless groundwater.

INLETS

Once water passes through the pump, it returns to the pool via the inlets. Rather than just allowing water to run back into the pool, inlets focus and concentrate the flow, jetting the water into the pool. This process helps distribute chemicals evenly and mixes heated water with cooler water to provide a uniform temperature.

Drains are required in all pools and spas to empty water periodically and draw water into the filter. A hydrostatic valve in the main drain allows groundwater to flow into an emptied pool, which prevents the shell from cracking or heaving out of the ground.

PUMPS

The electric pump in a swimming pool forms the mechanical center of the water circulation system. In a typical pump, an electric motor spins a blade called an impeller that drives water from the various pool drains through the filter, then back out into the pool through the inlets.

PUMP CAPACITY

In general, a pump should be able to circulate the entire volume of water in the pool at least once every 24 hours—and once every 8 hours is preferable to guarantee cleanliness. (The required circulation rate is often governed by local building codes, so check with your building department for specifics.) The volume of water flow depends on the diameter of the pipes in the plumbing system and the size of the motor powering the pump.

PIPE DIAMETER Most commonly, pipes that drain the pool measure 2 inches in diameter. Return pipes typically start at $1\frac{1}{2}$ inches but connect to smaller pipes of $\frac{3}{4}$ or even $\frac{1}{2}$ inch where they reach the inlets. This decrease in size increases the pressure, creating jets of water that help distribute chemicals and heat evenly.

Pumps vary in size according to the amount of water they have to circulate. A properly sized pump should be able to turn over the entire volume of water once every 8 to 24 hours.

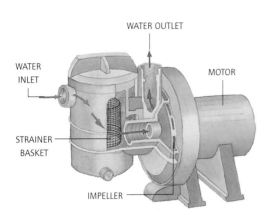

WATER OUTLET

WATER INLET

MOTOR

STRAINER BASKET

IMPELLER

MOTOR SIZE Usually, a 1.5-horsepower pump is sufficient. Many pool owners assume that a larger motor will move the water faster, but that isn't true. The flow of water is limited by the size of the pipes, so a larger pump will be working in vain to force water out faster. This puts it under heavy strain, which will seriously shorten its life. A properly sized pump might last 10 years or longer, but an oversized pump being strained might burn out after only three or four years. Also, an overworked pump is noisy. Matching the pump to the plumbing system requires careful calculation and is best left to a contractor.

Two-speed pumps are often used for spas. The higher speed is used to power the hydrojets. The lower speed operates the circulation through the filter and heater—and saves energy when the spa is not in use.

TIP

COST

For maximum efficiency, the pump should be installed no farther than 40 to 60 feet from the pool. Any farther than that will necessitate an increase in pump horsepower or the addition of a secondary booster pump to help send water back into the pool. Either way, it will add to the noise and to the expense.

FILTERS

A well-functioning filter is an essential element in maintaining water clarity, as it removes the nearly invisible particles that cause water to appear cloudy. Ordinary filtration systems do not remove bacteria, which is why chemical treatment is required as well (see pages 192–201).

CHOOSING THE RIGHT FILTER

There are many different types of filters, including high-rate sand filters, filters filled with pulverized material called diatomaceous earth, and cartridge filters, which are similar to the air filter in a car in both convenience and effectiveness. In the past, all three were viable choices for residential pools, but recent advances in cartridge filters have made them overwhelmingly preferred—about 99 percent of pool owners use a cartridge filter. A look at all the options will help explain why.

HIGH-RATE SAND FILTERS

Until recently, the high-rate sand filter was the most popular option for swimming pools. These filters contain pressurized tanks built of fiberglass, stainless steel, or plastic and are filled with special grades of sand that can trap particles as small as 5 microns (the typical human hair follicle measures between 40 and 120 microns thick). Water enters from the top, is forced to a drain at the bottom, then feeds back into the swimming pool. The pressurized system drives particles in the water deep into the sand bed.

Maintaining the filter of a pool or spa keeps the water fresh and inviting through the entire swimming season.

The drawback of these filters is that the sand they contain must be back-washed frequently in order to remove the particles and increase the efficiency of the filtering medium. While not a difficult task, backwashing does use a great deal of water—as much as 500 gallons per cleaning.

DIATOMACEOUS EARTH (D.E.) FILTERS

In these filters, water from the pool passes through filter grids coated with diatomaceous earth, a fine powder made from the chemically inert, fossilized remains of sea organisms called diatoms. Particles in the water catch on the edges of the D.E. and are held tight. D.E. filters are more compact than high-rate sand filters, since they do not contain a pressurized tank. More important, they filter out tinier particles—as small as 3 microns in diameter. But while these filters are effective, they also require backwashing, which again means using as much as 500 gallons of water each time. Worse, the diatomaceous earth itself is classified as a hazardous waste in many localities, and disposal is increasingly regulated.

CARTRIDGE FILTERS

Commercial and public swimming pools require high-rate sand or D.E. filters because they can clean very small particles out of the water. For residential pools, however, the best choice is a cartridge filter. The latest cartridge filters are almost as effective as high-rate

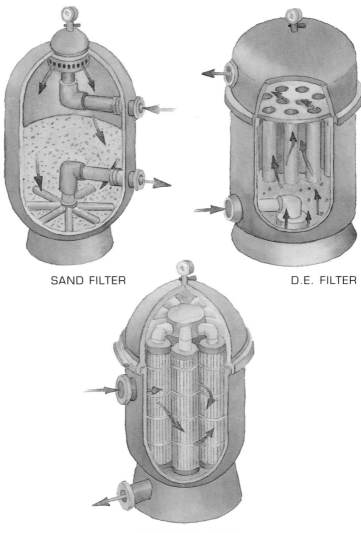

SAND FILTER

D.E. FILTER

CARTRIDGE FILTER

sand filters, trapping particles as small as 6 microns. They're also much easier and safer to maintain, and they require very little water for cleaning.

In a cartridge filter, water from the pool passes through a filter made of polyester cloth or corrugated paper. Instead of backwashing, you simply remove the filter and hose it off. After a few years, the filter will need replacing, but this is a simple process explained in the manufacturer's instructions.

HEATERS

Swimming pools should have a comfortable water temperature. The ideal temperature depends on your personal preference, but the range is usually between 78 and 82 degrees. Even in summer, the only way to guarantee that warmth is with a heater.

CHOOSING A HEATER

Pool heaters come in a number of styles based on the energy source they use. The cost to run the different types of heaters also varies widely, depending on the region you live in. Electricity, for instance, is far cheaper in some areas than in others. An experienced pool contractor will know which type of heater is the best value for your region.

GAS HEATERS

Gas heaters are the most popular type of pool heater because of the relatively low cost of the fuel. In addition, they are convenient and tend to heat water quickly because they use a direct flame. Gas heaters run on either propane or natural gas and are divided into three distinct types.

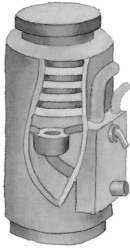

CONVECTION HEATER

CONVECTION HEATERS A large flame heats a steady stream of slow-moving water to a very high temperature. This type of heater is suitable for small pools and spas.

TANK HEATERS A small flame heats a large volume of water; it's cost-effective but not sufficient in cold climates.

COIL GAS HEATER

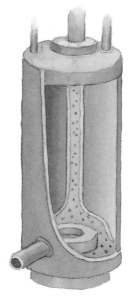

TANK HEATER

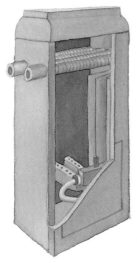

COIL HEATER

COIL, OR FLASH, HEATERS This is the most common type of gas heater. A large flame rapidly heats a coil through which a small but fast-moving stream of water passes. Although they are the most expensive type of heater because they consume the largest quantity of fuel, coil heaters are suited for pools and spas of any size, as they heat a large body of water quickly.

ELECTRIC HEATERS

Electric heaters, similar to those used for electric hot-water tanks in homes, heat water by emitting an electric current that produces heat in a coil. The coil warms a tank of water, a fairly slow process. While the purchase price of an electric heater is slightly lower than that of a propane or natural gas heater, the cost of electricity in most parts of the country makes these heaters the most expensive to use—and a poor choice.

ELECTRIC HEAT PUMPS

One way to use electricity wisely to heat a pool is to connect a water heater to a heat pump. Heat pumps operate on the same principle as air conditioners.

Refrigerants, heat exchangers, and compressors combine to transfer heat from one area to another rather than to generate heat.

But while an air conditioner transfers heat from inside to outside, a heat pump in a pool transfers heat from the air to the water. Warm outside air heats the refrigerant within the heat pump; it is then further heated and compressed by the compressor, resulting in a very hot gas. When the gas passes through a heat exchanger, its heat is transferred to the pool water.

The beauty of a heat pump is that although it runs on electricity, it actually yields many times more heat than could be produced by the same amount of electricity running an electric heater alone. The downside is that heat pumps work best in hot climates and are of little use in warming a pool in a northern climate during the spring and fall.

ELECTRIC HEAT PUMP

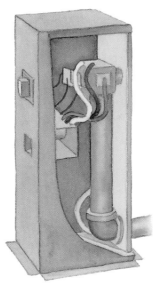

TIP

S M A R T

Because a heater is connected to the plumbing outside the pool, rather than to the piping within the pool, it is very easy to add a heater after the pool is built. If you're thinking of adding a heater sometime in the future, have all the necessary plumbing installed ahead of time.

GOING SOLAR

Because of the big expense of heating pool water, solar energy is an increasingly appealing option. The best way to ensure being able to trap solar energy is to site the pool well. If the pool has full southern or southwesterly exposure, with no shade from trees, then the water will heat up on its own, sometimes eliminating the need for supplemental heating entirely but in any case reducing heating costs.

USING SOLAR COLLECTORS

If more heat is needed than what the pool water alone can absorb, you can add solar collectors elsewhere. These devices are constructed simply and consist of a black metal plate with water-filled tubes running through it; the tubes are covered with clear acrylic to prevent loss of heat from wind. Pool water is warmed when the metal plate absorbs heat from the sun and transfers it to the water in the tubes, which flows back into the pool.

As a general rule, the surface area of solar collectors must add up to at least 75 percent of the surface area of the pool.

For example, if the swimming pool has a surface area of 400 square feet, you'll need 300 square feet of collectors. Solar collectors can be positioned anywhere on the property, but the most common location is on the roof of the house, facing directly south or slightly southwest.

A COMBINATION SYSTEM

Not all locations are ideally suited to using solar collectors, both because of the number of collectors needed and because the exposure has to be right. In addition, solar collectors do not work well in colder climates in the wintertime, for obvious reasons. Still, it is possible to produce at least some heat from solar collectors in many areas. A combination system will enable you to partially warm water through collectors, then warm it further with a conventional heater, reducing your overall heating bill.

WHAT SIZE HEATER?

The heating capacity of gas heaters is measured in British thermal units, or BTUs. A single BTU is defined as the amount of heat needed to raise the temperature of

Wisely sited solar collectors can result in substantial savings in the cost of heating a pool.

1 pound of water 1 degree Fahrenheit. The range of pool heaters goes from 20,000 BTUs to 200,000 BTUs and beyond. The size heater you need will depend on your geographic location as well as on how the pool will be used. If the goal is to add a few degrees of extra heat during the peak summer swim season, a small heater will suffice—possibly one that produces fewer than 50,000 BTUs. But if you want to extend the swim season year-round, you'll need a more powerful heater.

While calculations based on pool volume and the relative daytime and nighttime temperature averages can produce a BTU requirement, there are too many other variables, including wind conditions and water-cooling evaporation, to give you an exact number for your situation. It makes better sense to rely on the advice of an experienced contractor and to talk to friends and neighbors in order to arrive at a realistic heater capacity.

CALCULATING POOL VOLUME

TO SELECT AN APPROPRIATE HEATER, it's essential to know the volume of water in your pool. If your contractor cannot give you this information, you can estimate the number of gallons yourself. For a rectangular pool, multiply the length by the width by the average depth to determine the number of cubic feet. For a free-form pool, you may have to estimate the length and width, or break the pool into smaller segments and calculate each separately.

Once you have the volume in cubic feet, multiply that number by 7.48 (the number of gallons in 1 cubic foot of water) to yield the number of gallons in your pool. For example, a rectangular pool that is 20 by 40 feet and averages 6 feet deep will contain 4,800 cubic feet of water. This translates to more than 35,000 gallons of water.

TIP

SMART When installing solar collectors or combination systems, always choose a contractor who has a lengthy track record working with solar heat. While many contractors may think they can manage the simple technology, solar components require careful installation that only someone with experience should tackle. Choosing the right contractor will help avoid expensive mistakes.

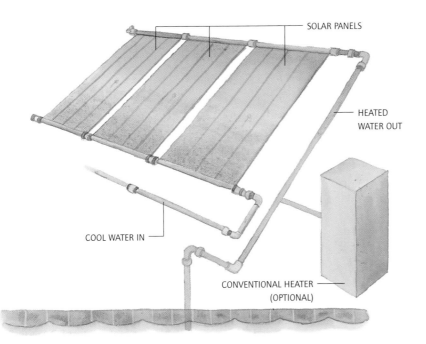

SOLAR PANELS

HEATED WATER OUT

COOL WATER IN

CONVENTIONAL HEATER (OPTIONAL)

housing the
EQUIPMENT

Pool equipment is usually built from plastic and other noncorrosive materials, allowing it to withstand the elements year-round. In most cases, all that is needed is a simple concrete pad for the equipment to rest on. However, pool owners often want to hide the equipment from view.

Equipment can be hidden behind a section of fencing, a simple hedge, or a small stand of evergreen trees or shrubs. Or the pool equipment can be housed in a separate shed, situated beneath a deck, or hidden from view entirely in an equipment room attached to a pool house or cabana. In addition to making the surroundings more pleasant, concealing the equipment can also help reduce noise from the pump.

OPPOSITE, TOP: This Cape Cod–style pool house has a small porch off the upstairs guest room that looks like the prow of a ship. Downstairs are a bathroom and storage for pool supplies.

OPPOSITE, BOTTOM: A small cedar building houses the mechanical equipment for an in-ground pool and spa. In addition to hiding equipment from view, the shed protects it from the weather and provides storage for chemicals and tools.

BELOW: Part of the attraction of this in-ground spa is its simplicity, with no equipment in sight. The wooden deck covers the spa workings, which can be accessed easily for maintenance through a hinged hatch.

TIP

If you're planning to house the plumbing, filtering, and heating equipment in one section of a pool house or cabana, proper ventilation is essential for a heater fueled with gas or propane. Ventilation will ensure that no fumes, in particular deadly carbon monoxide, can accumulate. To do the job right, have an experienced contractor set up the equipment, and be sure to install carbon monoxide detectors.

pool
COVERS

Pool covers keep maintenance to a minimum by protecting the water from debris. By reducing heat loss from evaporation and heat radiation, a cover can also lower heating bills substantially. Some models can even act as a safety device by supporting the weight of a person who falls on or walks across it.

COVERS FOR EASY MAINTENANCE

The simplest pool cover amounts to little more than a giant tarp that is stretched over the surface of an above-ground or in-ground pool. Such covers need to be firmly attached along the edges so they don't blow away in the wind. Special ties will anchor them, or the edges can be weighted down with sand- or water-filled bags. Many of the simplest covers are loose fitting. To prevent rainwater and snow from weighing them down, add

RIGHT: A loose-fitting energy-saving cover, maneuvered into place manually, reduces overnight heat loss.

BELOW: Strapped to the pool decking, this mesh cover is strong enough to walk on and allows water to filter through.

a floating ball beneath the cover, which will prevent precipitation from pooling. For maximum protection, make sure the cover extends at least 5 feet beyond the edge of an in-ground pool.

COVERS FOR ENERGY EFFICIENCY

During swimming season, a pool tends to gain heat from the sun during the day, then lose it at night through heat radiation as well as evaporation. If a pool is heated, covering it at night will reduce heat loss, resulting in not only warmer water but an energy savings of hundreds or even thousands of dollars over the course of a year. If a pool is unheated, covering it at night can mean that in the morning the water is comfortable rather than bone-achingly cold. Any cover, including a simple vinyl one, will help reduce heat loss. For added benefits, choose a solar cover, which contains air-filled baffles that increase the insulating value.

Covering your pool at night and during the off-season can reduce evaporation by up to 90 percent, which saves not only water but the energy used to heat it. You'll also need far less chemicals to treat the water, as it will stay cleaner.

TIP

SAFETY >

No matter which type of cover you use, be sure to remove it completely—rather than simply folding back a portion—before letting anyone use the pool. Swimmers can easily become trapped and disoriented if they surface beneath the cover.

COVERS FOR SAFETY

Tarps and solar covers offer no measure of safety. Anyone who steps or falls onto them will most likely end up in the water. Where safety is a primary concern, the best choice is a pool cover designed to withstand the weight of a person walking on it. These covers are made of a tough fiberglass mesh material and can hold loads of up to 400 pounds per square foot. When your pool is protected with this type of cover, you'll be able to use the pool deck and surrounding area year-round without having to worry about safety. (See more about safety covers on page 224.)

Because these safety covers are heavy, you'll want a track system, either manual or automatic, to help you cover and uncover the pool. If you plan to build a pool, it's best to incorporate a cover into your design if you want the cover to be as seamless as possible. With planning, the motor can be installed underground and the cover will slide along recessed tracks beneath the coping of the pool. When retracted, the cover will be practically invisible.

If you already have a pool, or if your pool has a unique shape, you'll probably need to install tracks that are either recessed into the deck or attached to its surface for the cover to glide along. These systems can be hand-cranked or automated. You can install a hand-cranked cover, which is less expensive, and upgrade later to an automated version. A motor can be installed either under the pool decking or in a nearby pool house or shed.

There are covers that can be customized for any shape of pool, even those with inte-grated water features or a vanishing edge. For zero-entry pools, where the water comes up to the lip of the edge, a flush-mounted track that abuts the overflow trough on two sides can be installed so that the cover blends seamlessly into the decking.

COST

Keep in mind that an automated pool cover is pricey. Installing one may cost between $8,000 and $12,000, compared with only a few hundred dollars for a simple vinyl maintenance cover. Consider all the factors before deciding what kind of cover is best for you, including the level of safety you require, whether children are ever present, and whether you're strong enough to take a cover off and put it back on every time you use the pool. And, of course, factor into the cover's price the money you'll save on heating and cleaning the water.

ABOVE: With the push of a button, an automatic cover glides on tracks hidden under the coping along the side of the pool. This type of cover is typically built in and can't be added later.

BELOW: It's possible to add a cover after the pool is built. This one runs along a deck-mounted track and is a good choice for odd-shaped pools.

ABOVE: Cover manufacturers can work with you to accommodate unique designs and vanishing-edge pools. In this example, the under-track system is completely out of sight when the cover is retracted, and the vanishing-edge effect is still visible even when the pool is covered. The spa has a matching cover.

pool CLEANERS

Even with main drains and skimmer baskets in your pool, debris is sure to accumulate, requiring additional cleaning. Handheld skimmers are one solution, but other devices can make the job much easier. Some of them are fully automatic, eliminating cleaning from your to-do list.

VACUUMS

Aquatic vacuums connect to the intake valve in the pool's skimmer basket, working off the pool's suction and filtration system to do their cleaning. Some vacuums are manual—you maneuver them across the pool bottom much as you'd vacuum the floor of a house. Automatic vacuums motor across the pool floor on their own. For above-ground pools that contain no skimmer baskets, consider getting a self-contained "robotic" vacuum that will clean the pool automatically. Run on rechargeable batteries, these units contain their own pumps, filters, and propulsion devices and just need to be placed in the pool to do the job.

SWEEPS

A sweep connects to one of the pool's inlets and uses the pressure of rushing water to power a tail that whips around the pool, dislodging debris. Some sweeps also capture debris and store it internally rather than sweeping debris into the main filter.

IN-FLOOR SYSTEMS

The ultimate accessory for an in-ground pool is an in-floor automatic vacuum system. Such a system can cost between $3,000 and $5,000 and is installed during pool construction. Underwater jets are built into the bottom of the pool and connected to the pool's return line. When the system is switched on, the heads pop up and a booster pump creates and forces out a high-pressure swirl of water. As the water moves along the floor of the pool, it produces a strong current that forces dirt and debris toward the main drains. There, the debris is siphoned out of the pool by the main pump and transported to the filtering system.

TIP

QUICK

With any type of aquatic cleaning system, be sure to clean the basket that collects large pieces of debris. If the basket becomes clogged, the system's vacuuming capability will be seriously reduced.

A vac-sweep (right) dislodges debris, then captures and stores it internally. A self-contained vacuum for an above-ground pool (above) uses batteries to operate its own pump and filter. An automatic pool vacuum (opposite) roves along the bottom of a pool, much like a vacuum inside a house.

pool
ACCESSORIES

At the top of the list of extras that can enhance your enjoyment of your swimming pool are practical accessories such as ladders and grab rails, purely recreational equipment such as slides and jump boards, and automatic controls that simplify maintenance.

LADDERS AND GRAB RAILS

In addition to built-in steps that ease swimmers into the shallow end, it's smart to install ladders and grab rails in the deep end of the pool. In fact, building codes frequently require both of these aids. Ladders and easy-to-grab railings give average swimmers a place to hold on to and rest during a swim and make it easier for all pool users to get in and out of the water.

Most ladders consist of three steps, two of which extend below the water level by about 2 feet. In general, the railings on these ladders are spaced between 18 and 24 inches apart, which allows swimmers to fit between them comfortably as they climb in or out. Entry steps that lead into the shallow end also benefit from having a railing. If the steps are wide, a single rail installed down the center works best. Ladders and railings require careful installation by an experienced contractor, as any mistake will cause them to wobble eventually.

As a pool safety device, horizontal rails installed just below

the water line are becoming increasingly common. These grab rails provide youngsters as well as physically challenged swimmers with a ready handhold if they tire, and they make the pool a safer place for everyone.

SLIDES

Pool slides are an increasingly popular recreational device. Though regulated and in some cases prohibited by local building codes, when properly installed

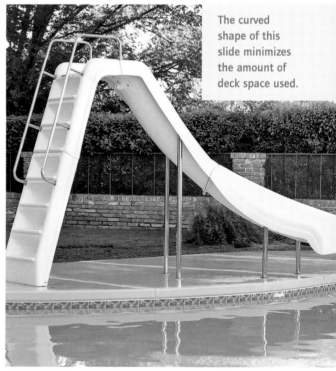

The curved shape of this slide minimizes the amount of deck space used.

they can be enjoyed without the safety concerns of diving boards.

You'll need to first make sure your pool is large enough and deep enough for a slide. An experienced contractor will be able to help you make that determination. In addition, the pool deck must be large enough to accommodate the slide. A large straight slide can measure more than a dozen feet from the ladder to the edge of the pool, but even a small slide can take up about 8 feet of deck space. Slides that curve or spiral take up less room and can actually be more enjoyable for swimmers to use, but whichever slide design you choose, proper attachment to the deck is critical to prevent mishaps. Most builders connect the slide to concrete either within or beneath the deck to ensure a sturdy base. Slides should never wobble, and they

ABOVE: A fully equipped swimming pool contains everything needed for recreation as well as safety—from slides to grab bars.

RIGHT: Grab rails positioned by steps minimize the risk of accidents.

should be inspected at once by a competent builder if they do.

Most slides are made from fiberglass and have a gel coating that provides an extra-slippery finish. Some pool builders create faux-rock slides that have a more natural look. Whatever style you decide on, be sure to have it constructed by an experienced builder.

DIVING BOARDS

Because they've fallen into disfavor with insurance companies as well as local building authorities, it is nearly impossible to add a spring-assisted diving board to most residential pools. In the few situations where they may be added, the size of the pool is the most important safety consideration. Though the exact dimensions will depend on the type of board being installed, pools should be a minimum of 8½ feet deep, 15 feet wide, and 28 feet long.

Diving boards are usually made of wood coated with fiberglass and covered with a nonskid surface. Maintaining the board is essential to safety. A warped surface or a crack in the material raises the possibility that the wood underneath has begun to rot. Replacement of the board is the only solution.

JUMP BOARDS

An alternative to adding a diving board to a new pool is to add a jump board. They are shorter and far safer than full diving boards—they're stationary rather than spring-loaded, so they don't launch a swimmer high into the air. Still, a pool must be large enough and deep enough to accommodate a jump board safely; local building codes do spell out the requirements, as do national standards (check with your pool builder for these). Unlike diving boards, most jump boards are made from aluminum—which creates a maintenance-free surface, although the nonskid coating may need occasional replacement or repair.

AUTOMATIC CONTROLS

Advances in technology have made swimming pools as easy to use and to maintain as turning on a TV. With the touch of a keypad, you can turn the pump on or off, adjust the heater, operate the automated cover, and switch on the lights. In addition, one touch will dispense chemicals that control water quality.

Jump boards provide a safer yet fun alternative to diving boards. Shorter and without the spring-loaded action of traditional diving boards, they lower the altitude that a diver gains—and thereby minimize the risk of mishaps.

AIR SWITCHES Since water and electronic controls don't mix well, one popular design for automated controls incorporates an air switch. Air switches can be used safely at poolside because the controls don't contain any electrical connections. Instead, when a button is depressed, it sends a pulse of air through a slender hose attached to a control that triggers an electronic switch nearby.

WIRELESS CONTROLS Systems that use radio frequencies (above) can be connected to the telephone, allowing homeowners to dial up the system while they are away so the temperature, lighting, and other features are ready when they arrive home.

ABOVE: Instead of choosing a traditional diving board, consider integrating your deck into the pool design. Ideal for a small yard, this deck overhangs the deep end of the pool so people can dive right in.

BELOW: Diving boards, such as this spring-loaded one, can add thrills to a swimming pool, but liability issues abound.

spa
BASICS

Despite its smaller size, a spa operates in much the same way as a swimming pool. A pump circulates the water, then passes it through a filter; the addition of chemicals destroys bacteria and keeps the water sterile.

HOW A SPA WORKS

Spas are generally heated to a much higher temperature than a swimming pool, and the force of the water flowing into the spa is much greater, producing the high-pressure rush of water that makes spas especially soothing.

When installed next to a swimming pool, an in-ground spa uses the same equipment as the pool itself. The pool's basic equipment needs to be slightly larger to handle the additional load. Freestanding spas require their own pump, filter, and heater. That equipment can be smaller than for a swimming pool, since the workload is smaller.

ABOVE: Tucked into the corner of a tranquil patio, this portable spa features a stone surround and wood coping.

LEFT: Natural-looking boulders blend this in-ground spa into the garden, and wide steps provide gentle access into the water.

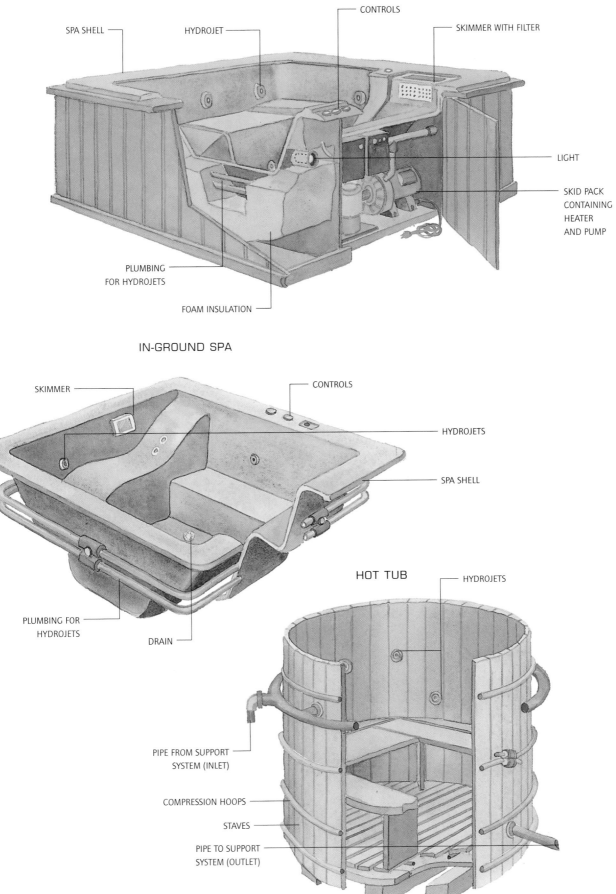

PORTABLE SPA

SPA SHELL

HYDROJET

CONTROLS

SKIMMER WITH FILTER

LIGHT

SKID PACK
CONTAINING
HEATER
AND PUMP

PLUMBING
FOR HYDROJETS

FOAM INSULATION

IN-GROUND SPA

SKIMMER

CONTROLS

HYDROJETS

SPA SHELL

PLUMBING FOR
HYDROJETS

DRAIN

HOT TUB

HYDROJETS

PIPE FROM SUPPORT
SYSTEM (INLET)

COMPRESSION HOOPS

STAVES

PIPE TO SUPPORT
SYSTEM (OUTLET)

HYDROJETS

Hydrojets propel water into a spa, providing the high-pressure massage action so prized by spa owners. A hydrojet mixes a pressurized stream of water with air, then forces it into the spa to create a bubbling swirl. Each hydrojet pumps out between 12 and 15 gallons of water per minute, and most spas contain at least four jets. Hydrojets do not have to be fixed in one orientation; in the best spa models, they move up and down to create a rippling massage. And in many spas, including prefabricated ones, you may be able to choose the exact location of the hydrojets. If you can, sit in the spa before you purchase it, so the hydrojets can be placed according to your preference.

Regulate the air intake on a hydrojet by opening or closing the ports near the top edge of the spa. When the ports are completely closed, hydrojets produce a gentle massage rather than a rippling one. With ports fully open, some models are able to spew out more than 75 gallons per minute, all through a single jet, to create an inviting whirlpool bath.

One drawback of hydrojets is that their blowers tend to be noisy. When a spa is inside the house, this can result in unbearable sound for everyone but the spa users. But when a spa is connected to an in-ground pool, blowers can usually be located far enough from the spa, with the other pool equipment, to minimize the impact of the noise.

SPA COVERS

A cover is an essential component of a spa, not just an option. First, covers provide safety by restricting access. Second, they keep out dirt and debris, which reduces the load on the pump and filter—especially important if the spa is outdoors. Another benefit a cover provides is energy savings. Keeping the spa covered when it's not in use will greatly reduce heat loss and therefore substantially reduce your energy bills.

RIGID COVERS tend to be made of vinyl-covered foam and provide the best insulation. Buy the highest-quality cover you

AIR INLET — WATER INLET —

FLOW
RESTRICTOR

HYDROJET
ACTION

can, because an inferior one will leak and become waterlogged. The thickness of covers varies, generally between 2 and 3 inches, and while the thinnest will suffice for indoors, the thicker models provide the best insulation for outdoor spas. Rigid covers are heavy, usually weighing 30 pounds or more, and can be difficult to maneuver.

ABOVE: In addition to rigid and flexible covers, there are custom options, such as this teak cover that slides on recessed tracks. When closed, the cover looks like a low-level deck.

BELOW: This rigid cover slides on tracks that were built into the spa and disappears out of sight when open.

FLEXIBLE COVERS provide a lightweight alternative. Some are filled with pockets of air that offer modest insulating value. While they offer little in the way of safety, they may suffice for your particular needs if your spa is fenced.

SPA HEATERS

While the ideal maximum temperature for a swimming pool is 78 to 82 degrees, spa water is heated much higher—in some cases, up to 104 degrees. Gas heaters are by far the fastest, warming the water in a matter of minutes. Among electric heaters, those that run on 110 volts heat water very slowly, while those that run on 220 volts are comparatively quicker. However, electric heaters are far more expensive to operate than gas heaters in most regions of the country.

SPA CONTROLS

Manual controls are ordinarily located right on the edge of the spa. They can be used to turn on the pump as well as the heater and the hydrojets, all with simple switches. Increasingly, however, spas can be adjusted from afar. Wireless controls allow adjustment from any room in the home. Telephone connections make it possible to control the settings from virtually anywhere, so you can arrive home to a spa that is heated, bubbling, and ready for use. No matter how sophisticated the controls, all spas have a manual override switch so you can make adjustments while you're in the spa.

CONSTRUCTION

IN THE FOLLOWING PAGES, you'll find the basic steps of pool and spa construction—when months of planning suddenly give way to the arrival of a work crew, a bulldozer, and a front-end loader and the project begins to take shape. Knowing what to expect during this period will help you track the process, allow you to preserve your patience, and help you feel certain that you're getting the pool or spa you want.

excavating an in-ground
POOL

Whether for a concrete, vinyl-lined, or fiberglass pool, the first step is similar to the construction of a house foundation. These pages can help you chart your contractor's progress and reassure you that you're making the right choices.

PREPARING FOR EXCAVATION

Before beginning construction of an in-ground pool, a contractor will need to clear a passage at least 10 feet wide to provide sufficient access for construction equipment. This may involve cutting down trees, removing fencing, and transplanting shrubbery. The access route will also need to have a firm enough base to provide traction for the machinery. In some situations, it may be necessary to truck in gravel or other stone to support the equipment, particularly if the construction site is on a steep slope.

STAKING OUT THE SITE

After preparing the access way, the contractor will lay out the exact site of the pool for excavation. First, the perimeter of the pool is staked out, which can be done in a variety of ways—from driving wooden stakes into the ground to dusting the outline with lime. In sloping yards where a portion of the pool wall will be built aboveground and then backfilled, plywood forms will be erected. From these forms you can get a good idea of how much filling and landscaping you'll be doing after construction.

ABOVE: The first stage of excavation for an in-ground pool involves large equipment. An excavator quickly digs the bulk of the hole needed.

OPPOSITE PAGE TOP: Experienced equipment operators can navigate even complicated pool layouts with precision. The curved wooden forms mark the free-form perimeter.

OPPOSITE PAGE BOTTOM: A finished pool bears no resemblance to the chaos of excavation. Good contractors make the most of a site's contours to create natural-looking settings.

TIP

S M A R T

Excavation is the most chaotic and potentially damaging part of pool construction. To lessen the impact on your yard, make all decisions with the contractor in advance, including exactly where the access route will be, the location for storing excavated soil, and which specific portions of your yard will be disturbed.

VINYL-LINED AND FIBERGLASS POOL EXCAVATION

Contractors normally begin excavation for a vinyl or fiberglass pool by using a backhoe or front-end loader to create a ramp through what will become the shallow end of the swimming pool. This allows them to move in and out of the pool with ease; when the job is finished, they will remove their equipment via the ramp.

The excavated hole will be between 6 and 12 inches bigger than the outside dimensions of the swimming pool. The additional width gives the contractor room to place the supporting walls for a vinyl-lined pool or the shell of a fiberglass pool. Once those are installed, the gap is then backfilled with sand, similar to the way a house excavation is backfilled once the concrete of the foundation walls has cured.

THE CONCRETE DIFFERENCE

In the case of a shotcrete or gunite pool, the excavation process is slightly different. Because the cuts into the earth become the forms for building the walls, they must be cut precisely in order to create the exact shape desired. If too much material is excavated, it will be difficult to build the pool as planned, because the walls can't be backfilled easily.

Rather than digging a hole larger than the pool and backfilling the gap when the walls are completed, the contractor, using heavy machinery, excavates a hole that is about 6 to 12 inches smaller than the pool's exterior walls. The final—and most critical—10 percent of cuts are then made by hand, with laborers using pickaxes, shovels, and other hand equipment to loosen and cart away material. This handwork tends to make excavations for shotcrete or gunite pools more expensive than those for fiberglass or vinyl-lined pools.

MANAGING WET SOIL

One of the biggest problems encountered during swimming pool construction is groundwater. Any site where standing water is an issue is not a good candidate for a pool. But even where the ground appears dry, digging a hole 5 or 6 feet into the earth can sometimes yield water. This bogs down machinery and can make it difficult—though not impossible—for work to continue.

Where water is a problem, contractors will sometimes dig about 12 inches deeper into the floor of the pool than originally planned. They then add drainage piping to the floor, backfill the floor with loose gravel, and add a sump pump that connects to the drainage piping. The pump allows enough water to be drawn from the area to improve working conditions without compromising the future shape of the pool.

TIP

TIME

To avoid delays caused by waterlogged soil, it's better to excavate a pool in drier months, when the water table is lower.

ABOVE: After a concrete in-ground pool is excavated with machinery, workers have to fine-tune the hole the old-fashioned way—with picks and shovels.

LEFT: For a vinyl-lined pool, the hole is excavated entirely with heavy equipment. It is then lined with sand to create a smooth, stable surface for the liner.

building concrete
POOLS

Concrete pools made from gunite or shotcrete require more labor and involve more details than the alternatives. The following pages describe the sequence of steps that are needed after excavation is complete.

LAYING THE FRAMEWORK

While concrete has a great deal of strength, it has little elasticity and cracks easily under stress. The most common way to address this weakness is to combine concrete with a framework of steel reinforcement rods (rebar). The result is a structure that's strong and resilient.

Once excavation is complete, contractors place the rebar. The placement and amount will vary according to the project, but in general rebar is laid in an evenly spaced cross pattern to ensure uniform strength throughout. Intersecting pieces are tied together with wire to create a giant steel grid that forms the skeleton of the pool.

After the rebar is placed and tied, the plumbing system is positioned, complete with pipes connecting to the main drains and the inlets. These pipes will become embedded in the concrete when it is applied, so it is crucial for them to be positioned well—it will be nearly impossible to make changes

In-ground pools built of concrete (in the form of shotcrete or gunite) allow the greatest versatility and originality in design. This elaborate pool and raised spa could be achieved only with this material.

During construction of an in-ground pool, the excavated shape becomes the mold for the pool itself. Steel reinforcement rods, known as rebar, combine with shotcrete or gunite to give the walls resilience.

later. To discover any plumbing leaks before the shotcrete or gunite is applied, a good pool contractor fills the pipes with pressurized air and monitors the pressure during construction.

The wiring is also installed at this time. Rather than embed it directly in concrete, most electricians will install a piping system known as conduit through which they thread the wiring. This way, if any repairs are needed in the future, new wiring can simply be pulled through the conduit, without the need for excavation or jackhammering.

CROSS-SECTION OF A CONCRETE POOL

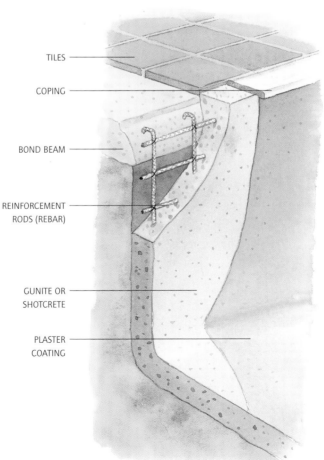

TILES

COPING

BOND BEAM

REINFORCEMENT RODS (REBAR)

GUNITE OR SHOTCRETE

PLASTER COATING

APPLYING SHOTCRETE OR GUNITE

While the foundation for a house is poured with the help of forms that mold the concrete into a specified shape, creating a gunite or shotcrete swimming pool is a more free-form process—the material is sprayed on and hand-troweled into shape. Before spraying begins, the drains and inlet openings are covered to keep them from being plugged up.

Ideally, the floor is sprayed first, followed by the walls. Some contractors spray the walls first, then trowel anything that spills to the floor as the base, but that's less desirable. The reason is that gunite and shotcrete become stronger when they are pressure applied, as opposed to simply being troweled into place. It is very important that the material be directed behind the rebar and against the earth so that pockets of air or loose soil cannot form and weaken the shell.

An experienced contractor will usually start with the floor, working in one small area of the pool at a time, perhaps a section as small as 4 by 4 feet. The work most often begins in the middle of the pool, then spreads out toward the sides. When the floor is finished, the contractor will work up the sides of the walls. If any material falls to the floor, it can be troweled into place without weakening the overall structure, because any air pockets beneath it will already have been eliminated. Shotcrete and gunite harden fairly quickly, and they can be walked on within three to four hours after they have been applied.

BELOW: Both shotcrete and gunite are applied to the rebar with a high-pressure spray. This eliminates air pockets that might otherwise form in the walls, which would seriously weaken them.

RIGHT: A pool made of concrete has a permanence unmatched by any other material. It can last for decades and can be replastered and even renovated.

JUDGING QUALITY BY THICKNESS

Gunite and shotcrete need to be built up in layers rather than applied in one burst. The final thickness averages between 6 and 9 inches. The bond beam, which forms the topmost portion of the wall of the pool just beneath the coping, will be thicker still, perhaps 12 to 14 inches. This gives the walls additional stability by uniting the various layers of concrete, rebar, and undisturbed soil into one permanent block.

The preferred thickness of shotcrete and gunite depends on the climate as well as the nature of the surrounding soil. In climates where the ground freezes in winter, a thickness of at least 9 inches is needed. In warmer climates that have no winter freeze, a thickness of about 6 inches should be sufficient, but check any local regulations.

In either case, the concrete has to cure, or completely harden, before it can be used, a process that can take between two and three weeks. For the first three to four days, it requires gentle hosing several times a day to keep it wet. This prevents small shrinkage cracks that can form in the surface.

ADDING TILING

After the walls have cured, the finishing process begins. Often, the top portion of the pool wall is lined with tile rather than plastered, since evaporating water can leave marks that are easier to clean off of tile than off of plaster. Tiling is also decorative, with countless possible styles and effects. If you use tile, be sure to add it only after the concrete has fully cured. Otherwise, some tiles may work themselves loose as the wall shrinks slightly.

ADDING COPING

Once tile has been added, the next step is to install the coping, the layer of material that forms a transition between the pool and the surrounding deck or lawn. The coping often consists of concrete blocks or natural stones, which are laid on top of the wall and tilted at a slight angle or have a curve carved into them. The angle or curve will prevent runoff water from draining into the pool.

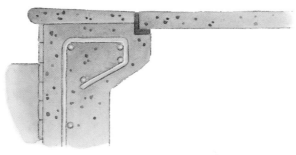

The material used to create the coping can be different from that of the surrounding deck (above), or the same (below).

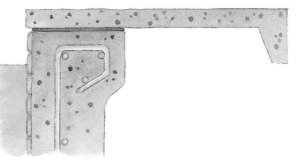

PLASTERING THE POOL

The final step is to plaster the walls with a hand trowel. Plaster is usually applied from the bottom of the pool up to the top in small sections, similar to the way gunite and shotcrete are applied. Plaster is feathered up toward the tile to form an even surface that matches the tile in thickness.

Plaster can be applied only to walls that are completely cured. Any attempt to put it on sooner will likely fail, because the plaster may crack and begin to disintegrate as the concrete underneath cures. In addition, the walls that the plaster is being applied to must be completely dry. If there is any moisture on the walls—from recent rainfall or heavy dew, for example—the plaster will slough from the surface as it's applied.

Plaster can be applied in its natural pure-white state, or color or tiny grains of marble or granite can be added to the mix. No matter which color or material

When a tile rim is installed around the perimeter of the pool, it is added before the walls are plastered. This ensures that the two surfaces will match up seamlessly when the plaster is applied.

TIP

S M A R T

When filling a freshly plastered pool, make sure the water flows in steadily. If it stops and the pool is allowed to sit partially filled, an indelible mark will stain the uncured plaster all around the pool. Tiling the top portion of the swimming pool just beneath the coping will prevent any water marks, since the water level can stop at the tile rather than on the fresh plaster.

LEFT: Because concrete pools are hand-fabricated, they can be completely customized. This allows for unique features to be added, such as this vividly patterned tiled surface.

BELOW: An area of the pool that rises above water level is a great place to make a statement with tile.

you use, the mixture must be blended carefully so the pool has a consistent appearance from one area to another. Plaster dries very quickly, in about 30 minutes or even less, but complete curing takes about 30 days. In order to cure properly, plaster on a pool wall needs to be submerged completely in water. This means that the pool will have to be filled—a process that is covered on page 132. The pool will need to stay filled for the entire curing period.

building vinyl-lined
POOLS

Vinyl-lined pools cost significantly less than concrete pools because of the reduced costs of the prefabricated materials and the simpler construction techniques. Rather than taking a month or more to complete, a vinyl-lined pool can be assembled in a matter of days after excavation.

CONSTRUCTING THE POOL WALLS

Once excavation is completed, the perimeter of the pool is filled with concrete to form footings. These are exactly analogous to footings that support concrete foundation walls in a house. When the concrete is dry, the footings are leveled and the sidewalls from the pool manufacturer are bolted together and anchored in place. Sidewalls, made from aluminum, fiberglass, plastic, pressure-treated wood, or other materials, can be erected and sometimes braced around the perimeter of the pool in just a few hours.

With the sidewalls in place, plumbing for the main drains, skimmers, return inlets, and automatic cleaners is installed on the walls' exterior, along with any lighting or other electrical systems. The bracing that supports the sidewalls is then covered with sand or earth that was excavated from the construction site. No curing time is needed for a vinyl-lined pool.

Once the pool walls are erected and a smooth base is prepared, the liner is set into place and attached to the tops of the walls. Since the liner arrives in one large piece, installing it is fairly quick.

INSTALLING THE LINER

Instead of plaster and concrete, a vinyl-lined pool incorporates a continuous piece of vinyl to create a watertight seal. To install one correctly, the floor of the swimming pool is usually covered with sand to create a smooth surface for the liner. The liner is then lowered into position, stretched taut, and fastened to the tops of the sidewalls just beneath the area where the coping will be installed. After cutting openings to accommodate drains, skimmers, inlets, and lights, the contractor assembles the plumbing and electrical systems. As the pool is filled with water, the contractor smoothes the liner.

Because of their ease of installation, vinyl-lined pools cost significantly less than concrete pools. When they're designed well, however, the overall look can be every bit as appealing.

CROSS-SECTION OF A VINYL-LINED POOL

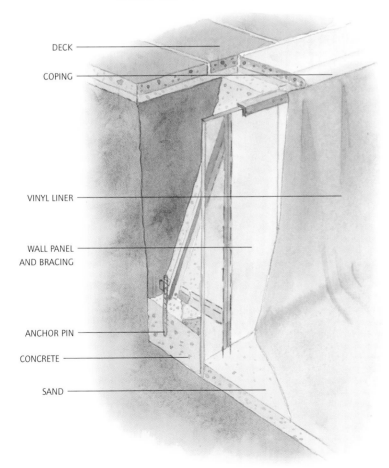

DECK
COPING
VINYL LINER
WALL PANEL AND BRACING
ANCHOR PIN
CONCRETE
SAND

TIP

DESIGN

The liners themselves are the decorative focal point of vinyl-lined pools. They come in a variety of colors and patterns, including tile motifs, that mimic the more expensive finishes of concrete pools.

building fiberglass
POOLS

Fiberglass pools are popular because of the ease of construction. They come preformed and prefinished and are simply set into the ground with the help of a crane.

CONSTRUCTION STEP BY STEP

After excavation, the electrical system and rough plumbing go in. Then sand is spread in the bottom of the hole and contoured to conform to the shape of the pool shell. Using a crane, the installer lifts the shell off the truck and lowers it into position. Normally, some leveling and adjustment are required to position the shell just right, which may involve removing it and adding sand.

Once the shell is positioned correctly, the contractor holds it in place with temporary bracing made of long pieces of wood and large metal clamps.

Fiberglass pools come in an assortment of imaginative designs. These can be augmented by creative additions, such as the three water features shown here.

Next, the final plumbing and electrical connections are made. After this, the pool is filled with water at the same time it's backfilled with a slurry of sand and water to help eliminate pockets of air. It is essential that the two processes take place simultaneously. The water helps hold the pool in place and keeps the backfill from pressing against the side of the pool and caving it in.

The enormous shell of a fiberglass pool is hauled to a construction site on a flatbed truck and will later be set into place with a giant crane.

CROSS-SECTION OF A FIBERGLASS POOL

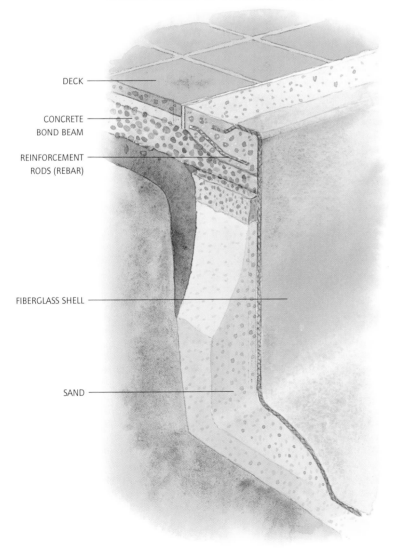

DECK

CONCRETE BOND BEAM

REINFORCEMENT RODS (REBAR)

FIBERGLASS SHELL

SAND

TIP

DESIGN

Vinyl-lined and concrete pools require a 10-foot-wide clearance for machinery, and a fiberglass pool requires even more room. Because the entire pool is delivered to your yard, not only does it need to fit in the pool site, but there needs to be enough room to allow a crane to lower the pool into place. Before ordering a fiberglass pool, check with a contractor to make sure your yard can accommodate it.

installing above-ground
POOLS

Above-ground pools range from small inflatable versions that can barely hold a family of four to large models that can comfortably fit a large crowd. While you can set up a small pool by simply following the manufacturer's instructions, larger above-ground pools are far more complicated.

Large above-ground pools may require site preparation as well as careful installation. Tempting as it may be to assemble one by yourself in the hope of saving money, it is almost always better to hire a professional installer to do the task. It eliminates problems and ensures that your pool warranty remains in effect.

PREPARING THE SITE

Unlike in-ground swimming pools, above-ground pools do not require extensive excavation before they are placed in a yard. Nevertheless, they do have to be installed on level ground

to maintain their structural integrity. This preparation often involves grading with heavy equipment. To properly create a level site, all grass and roots must be stripped away to expose the bare soil. Then you must level the ground again by scraping the soil down so that it is even with the lowest spot in the area. (Although it's easier to fill the lowest

Construction of an above-ground pool begins with excavation—although on a smaller scale than for an in-ground pool. Below, the topsoil is stripped away and the surface is graded to create a level site, which will reduce the possibility of settling over time.

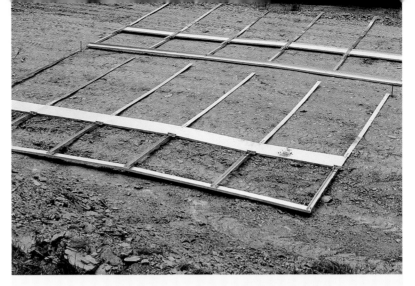

spots with enough soil to match the highest spots, this solution creates problems. Over time, it generally leads to uneven settling, which may weaken the pool structure.) After the surface is leveled, contractors usually spread a 6-to-12-inch layer of sand over the soil. This provides a firm base for the pool and prevents anything sharp from puncturing the surface of the delicate pool liner.

ABOVE: When the site is graded and level, the base of the frame is assembled in place where the pool will be installed.

ASSEMBLING THE POOL SYSTEM

While the details for installing an above-ground swimming pool vary from manufacturer to manufacturer, several key steps are common to all brands. Most swimming pools are created first with a piece known as a bottom rail placed along the ground around the perimeter of the pool. This metal track serves as a mini-foundation for the wall panels that will form the sides of the pool. Wall panels can be made from numerous materials, including aluminum, fiberglass, and plastic.

ABOVE: After the frame is assembled, the center is filled with sand, which provides a soft yet stable base to hold the pool liner.

BELOW: Above-ground siding supports, which will hold the pool walls upright, are positioned once the base is readied.

Round pools tend to be self-supporting, but oval-shaped pools need additional support on the sidewalls to prevent them from caving in when the pool is filled. The braces come in many styles. In addition, some pools are built of wood panels that fit together tongue-and-groove style for added strength. Such pools can be further supported by a metal band that circles them, similar to the hoop that holds together a wooden hot tub.

ABOVE: When the above-ground supports are in place, the sidewalls are attached, forming the basic shape of the pool.

ABOVE: With the sidewalls attached, additional supports are added on the exterior to buttress the walls against the weight of the water.

BELOW: Once the pool is stabilized, the vinyl liner can be attached to the tops of walls and smoothed so that it is free of air pockets.

INSTALLING THE LINER

Once the sidewalls are erected, the sand on the floor must be carefully smoothed and leveled. The usual method is to sweep a straight 2 by 4 in circles around the pool's interior with the help of a level. The vinyl liner is then installed in a manner similar to that used for a vinyl-lined in-ground pool. The liner is fastened temporarily to the tops of the sidewalls, then carefully worked into proper position. When it is in place, the pool is filled with water from a garden hose. As it fills, the contractor stretches the liner taut and fastens it more securely to the tops of the walls. It's important to remove all air pockets, folds, and wrinkles, as these create surfaces that can be punctured more easily than flat ones. For further protection, some pool manufacturers suggest sur-

rounding the exterior of the pool with a 6-inch-wide ring of sand, which helps reduce the risk of punctures from the outside, especially those that might be caused by trimmers and lawn mowers.

INSTALLING THE PLUMBING AND ELECTRICAL SYSTEMS

With the liner in place, the pool's plumbing and electrical systems can be added. In most above-ground pools, precut areas are ready for the skimmers. For maximum effectiveness, pumps and other equipment, which tend to be small for above-ground pools, should be located right next to the pool. However, be certain they're kept out of the entrance path to the pool. For best results, follow the instructions' placement advice carefully.

ABOVE: Mechanical equipment for an above-ground pool sits beneath the deck.

BELOW: The finished above-ground pool is a structure that is as eye-catching as it is sturdy.

remodeling a concrete
POOL

One of the advantages of shotcrete and gunite pools, compared with vinyl and fiberglass alternatives, is that they can be remodeled. You can do a simple makeover or a complete coping-to-floor-drain rehab that dramatically alters the way the pool functions.

THE SIMPLEST MAKEOVER

A concrete swimming pool can be reborn simply with new decking and coping material. First, the tile and top 12 inches of plaster are chiseled out, then new coping and tile are installed. When everything is set, new plaster is applied to the top portion of the wall and carefully feathered in so that the new surface and the old blend seamlessly.

Depending on the type of material used for the deck and coping, this sort of project might cost between $5,000 and $8,000—well worth it, since it can vastly enhance the look of a dated swimming pool.

The straight edges of these massive flagstone pieces give the remodeled deck a more formal look. The designer used smaller flagstone tiles on the coping to tie the pool and the deck together.

ABOVE: A new water feature can update the look of an older concrete pool. This low retaining wall hides the waterfall equipment and creates a natural-looking backdrop for the cascading water.

LEFT: Even if you don't want to change the deck material, installing tile coping and edging the steps with tile can add color and change the look of the pool inexpensively.

TIP

SMART

Concrete swimming pools are remarkably resilient and can be remodeled in just about all cases—even when the walls and plaster are severely cracked and don't hold water. In such cases, a fiberglass coating can be applied to create a lasting, watertight surface on top of the old one.

129

AN EXTENSIVE MAKEOVER

More extensive digging and chipping away can produce a thorough remodel of a concrete swimming pool. Such a makeover can involve digging along the sidewalls to attach plumbing systems for new returns and new drains, as well as upgrading equipment such as skimmers and lighting. Walls can also be raised to deepen the pool, in combination with exterior grading. In addition, natural-rock formations, waterfalls, spillways, and integral spas can be added fairly easily.

COST-BENEFIT ANALYSIS

A major swimming pool renovation is not cheap. In fact, when all the work is done, it may cost nearly as much as building an entirely new swimming pool. So why should you bother with remodeling? Not only is it

ABOVE: Adding submerged natural rock edging to this pool was a major renovation that cost a lot in time and money, but it was still cheaper than starting over from scratch.

LEFT: One of the best ways to give a concrete pool a new look is to choose an alternative to a smooth plaster finish. One that contains small bits of marble, granite, or pebbles, such as this example, can also provide more traction on steps.

more environmentally responsible, but in many cases it still makes financial sense for one simple reason. In order to build a new pool, the old pool has to be demolished. This is an expensive proposition because it includes not just the cost of labor but the extremely high cost of disposing of the heavy debris. A 16-by-32-foot rectangular pool might cost between $10,000 and $12,000 to demolish and cart away—a large amount to add to the cost of a new pool.

In addition, you will be building in what is known as disturbed or filled soil. This requires special engineering as well as additional footings, thicker walls, and more steel rebar—all of which will require more money.

If you already have a concrete swimming pool and want to change it radically, the best thing to do is engage in a top-to-bottom renovation.

BELOW AND RIGHT: A landscape architect gave this old pool new life. The pool was replastered, and 2-inch Pennsylvania blue stone coping matches the new deck. Plantings of nepeta and roses soften the edges of the stone, while potted petunias add more color. With all these changes, plus new fencing around the pool, it looks like a completely different yard.

BEFORE

AFTER

filling pools with
WATER

Pools require a great deal of water to fill. The average volume for an in-ground pool is about 20,000 gallons. An above-ground pool about 15 feet in diameter can contain 5,000 gallons, and a 20-by-40-foot rectangular pool can require as much as 35,000 gallons, depending on the depth.

FILLING A GUNITE OR SHOTCRETE POOL

A freshly plastered concrete pool needs to be filled immediately with water. Otherwise the plaster surface may crack and shrink and need to be recoated. But filling the pool has to be done carefully to avoid staining the walls.

A gunite or shotcrete pool lined with plaster should be filled from the bottom, usually with a hose placed at the base of the pool. When you are filling the pool, it is important to add the water consistently, not stopping until it reaches the tile border just beneath the coping. If a pool is filled in fits and starts, there will be pronounced high-water lines etched into the plaster walls. If water is trucked into the pool rather than run in from a garden hose, it should be pumped in through a hose placed at the base of a wall rather than splashed down the pool sides. Splashing it will make permanent marks on the pool walls.

Swimming pools are infrequently emptied once they've been filled. But in some climates pools can lose between 1 and 2 inches of water per day, requiring daily refilling. A pool cover can drastically reduce evaporation.

While the landscaping, decking, and outdoor furniture are important design elements, the main focus of a pool is the glistening water. Adding the sound of moving water only enhances the experience.

FILLING A VINYL-LINED OR FIBERGLASS POOL

Pools made of these materials require less care during filling. They don't need to be filled immediately—although it's a good idea for safety's sake—and there's no risk of staining if water happens to run down the sides. Therefore, it's not necessary to place the hose in the bottom of the pool. It can simply hang over the side and be allowed to run.

AVOIDING EXCESS WATER FEES

The most convenient way to fill a swimming pool is to turn on a hose and let it flow. Depending on the rate of flow and the size of the swimming pool, filling can take between one and several days. Often, communities will charge separate fees for water usage and for sewer use—disposing of the water. In order to avoid this double charge, which can amount to hundreds of dollars for a large swimming pool, check to see if your community allows a diversion meter to be installed in your plumbing supply system. Such a meter measures the water and waste flows separately so that you're charged only for what goes into the pool. In many cases, the cost of installing a diversion meter is more than offset by the reduction in the disposal fee.

OPTING FOR TANKED-IN WATER

If your home is supplied by a well pump, the task of filling a swimming pool may put too much strain on your system. In this case—and in many cases where local water restrictions are in effect—it may make sense to have water brought in by a tanker truck. The fee can actually turn out to be less than the cost of water from a municipal system combined with a sewer charge. The price of trucked-in water varies, but on average it costs about $35 per 1,000 gallons, or $350 for a 10,000-gallon pool.

TIP

COST

Water usage fees vary from municipality to municipality and can greatly affect the cost of filling a swimming pool. Check in advance with your local office about any discounts available to swimming pool owners to make sure you get the lowest possible rate.

spa construction
BASICS

In nearly every detail, the construction of an in-ground spa, whether concrete or acrylic, mirrors that of an in-ground swimming pool. Likewise, a portable spa has much in common with an above-ground swimming pool, especially in preparing the site before positioning the pool.

CONCRETE SPAS

Right down to the smallest feature, a shotcrete or gunite spa is built the same way as an in-ground pool made of the same material. As with a pool, about 90 percent of the hole for the spa has to be machine-excavated, with the remaining 10 percent dug by hand. When that is done, a grid built of steel reinforcement rod is assembled to form the spa skeleton. The rebar is also used to create any steps or benches the spa will contain. When this work is completed, the plumbing, including the drains and inlets for the hydrojets, and the electrical wiring are attached.

Next, the gunite or shotcrete is applied under pressure, sprayed directly against the rebar so that all pockets of air are eliminated. When the spraying is completed, the material is troweled smooth and allowed to cure for several weeks. The next step is either tiling or applying a layer of plaster to form the surface coating. As with swimming pools, coping material is usually placed along the top of the spa, to create a transition to the deck and surrounding landscape.

BELOW: A spa complements an in-ground pool in every way. Its warmer water provides a welcome haven from the cooler water of the pool, and its scale creates an intimate zone for relaxation.

ABOVE AND BELOW: The simplest way to build a spa is to include one during construction of an in-ground pool. This lessens the construction costs compared with building one separately, and it ensures that construction will proceed smoothly, without damaging the main pool.

IN-GROUND ACRYLIC AND FIBERGLASS SPAS

Installing an in-ground acrylic or fiberglass spa is nearly identical to installing a fiberglass swimming pool, although far less effort is needed because of the spa's significantly smaller size. Get the guidance of a contractor or an engineer to determine the right spot to site the spa. The excavated hole will be slightly larger than the spa in all directions. When the excavation is complete, the hole is lined with sand that is molded to conform to the shape of the spa. It is essential that no pockets of air exist when the spa is set in place, to keep the spa shell from caving in and ultimately developing leaks. Once the spa is in place, the electrical and plumbing systems can be installed. Then the gap between the hole and the spa should be backfilled with sand to provide firm support.

ADDING A SPA TO AN EXISTING POOL

When you are adding a spa to an existing swimming pool—whether concrete, vinyl-lined, or fiberglass—there are several factors to consider. First, the spa cannot be built directly adjacent to the pool, nor can the wall of the existing pool be cut into to any significant degree. If either of these is done, the pool's structure can become compromised and may even collapse. Instead, the spa needs to be built away from the pool wall by at least 2 feet. An engineer or experienced contractor should determine the exact location. However, the spa can still be connected to the pool via a spillway or waterfall, providing an integrated appearance without weakening the pool's

Portable outdoor spas offer easy mobility. Because of their weight when filled, they require firm support from underneath, often in the form of a concrete, gravel, or sand base.

An in-ground spa can easily be added to an existing pool—provided construction does not weaken the pool's structure. A contractor can best determine how close it can safely be located to the existing pool.

TIP

COST

If you have an existing concrete pool, you can probably add an acrylic spa for a fraction of the cost of a gunite or shotcrete spa. Despite the difference in materials, the new spa can be connected to the main pool's electrical and plumbing systems.

structure. In most cases, the spa can be connected to the pool's plumbing and electrical systems fairly easily, though this is also a job for an experienced contractor.

INSTALLING A PORTABLE SPA

Portable spas are easy to set up but require special care to guarantee long life and to ensure that the manufacturer's warranty remains in effect. For outdoor installation, the spa will need to be placed on either a concrete platform (see page 41) or a 6-to-12-inch bed of sand on carefully leveled soil.

If a spa is positioned on a deck or porch, its tremendous weight may have to be supported by a system of posts and piers. Be sure to consult a contractor or an engineer to make certain the spa poses no danger. Portable spas can also be installed indoors, in which case it's essential to choose an appropriate location (see page 40).

FILLING A SPA

Spas are easily filled with a garden hose. They lose slightly less water to evaporation than swimming pools because of their smaller surface area, but they may need water added two to three times a week to remain full. Putting on a cover can dramatically reduce evaporation.

LANDSCAPING

A WELL-CRAFTED POOL or spa deserves an equally attractive and well-planned setting, whether you're creating your landscape from scratch or redoing one that's been in place for years. That most likely means including walls or fences to ensure safety and privacy, as well as decorative gardens, patios, decks, walkways, water features, and lighting systems—not to mention places to store all the needed maintenance gear.

planning your
LANDSCAPE

Every successful landscape design begins with a single question: What do I want from this space? Although the specific answers vary, there are several broad goals that apply to the setting for any pool or spa. Start by considering these basic aims and deciding where each one falls on your list of priorities.

AESTHETICS

It's true that beauty is in the eye of the beholder, and it's also true that beauty is far more important to some people than to others. For instance, to some pool owners, all that really matters is a good swim (spa owners may just want a nice long soak in a hot tub). These people are not much concerned with how well the particular body of water suits its setting. At the other extreme are people who rarely take a dip. Their pleasure comes from the sight of an elegant pool blended seamlessly with its surroundings. Chances are you fall somewhere between those two opposites. But where? Your answer will determine not only the details of your landscaping plan but also how long you're willing to wait for it to be completed.

OPPOSITE PAGE: A border of perennials brightens up a simple rectangular pool.

BELOW: This two-tiered landscape is ideal for entertaining. While dining on the upper deck, guests can look down on the pool and spa below. A mixture of ground covers and trees softens the look of such a large paved area.

CONVENIENCE AND FLEXIBILITY

Consider all the pool-related activities on your agenda, such as cooking and eating, entertaining, showering, and changing. Also consider how many people might be involved in these functions. Then incorporate into your plan all the areas or structures required to handle your needs. Try to place these facilities close to the pool or spa.

When space is tight, your sanity-savers will be landscape elements that do multiple jobs—for instance, benches that also store furniture, sports gear, or garden tools; or a fire pit whose cover converts it to a low table or extra seating. Easy access to your pool from more than one part of your house will provide flexibility but may require an alarm or self-locking doors if small children are on the scene.

ALL IN GOOD TIME

NO LAW SAYS you have to install your entire landscape in one fell swoop—especially if you're undecided about such factors as the kind of paving you want for your pool deck or whether to use a wall, fence, or hedges to gain privacy. Why rush into something you may regret, or even wind up tearing out a few years down the road? Here are some ideas for temporary solutions to long-term goals.

- Have your pool installed in your lawn with just a broad coping and leave the decking for later. Just be careful when you mow, so that grass clippings don't end up in the water.

- Erect whatever safety fencing the law and your peace of mind require, but improvise on privacy screens. For example, inexpensive wire mesh covered with annual vines; stands of tall, bushy, fast-growing annuals; or freestanding screens, with or without plants, will all provide seclusion while you debate the merits of other, more permanent options.

- Let a pavilion or other large shade structure wait until next year—or even the year after. In the meantime, shield loungers from the sun with patio umbrellas or colorful canvas panels attached to tall stakes.

SAFETY

Safety is the top priority in any pool landscaping scheme. Many communities mandate security fencing as well as self-closing, self-latching, self-locking gates. (Even where these features are not required by law, your mind will rest easier with them in place.) Passageways near the pool need to be well defined and unobstructed, with firm traction and good lighting. (See more about safety on pages 216–225.)

PRIVACY AND COMFORT

As is the case with aesthetics, people vary quite a bit in their thoughts about privacy. If it ranks near the top of your priority list, include fences, walls, dense trees, or hedges in your plan, to block the view of your pool or spa from anyplace outside your yard. Depending on your climate, you may also want to add structures or plantings that block intense sun and wind—or you may need to remove shade-casting obstacles in order to provide more warmth.

EASE OF MAINTENANCE

With maintenance costs rising, and your own time at a premium, you'll want to choose your landscaping palette carefully. Easy-care winners include masonry surfaces that need no painting, rustproof and water-resistant furniture, and plants that thrive naturally in your climate while dropping a minimum of leaves, flowers, and fruit.

OPPOSITE PAGE, TOP: Privacy is not a concern in this backyard, where the pool is shrouded in dense trees.

OPPOSITE PAGE, BOTTOM: Tiled chairs that can be hosed off are easy to maintain, and they add a unique look to the pool area.

BELOW: An iron gate is the only entry point to this walled pool area. The gate is self-closing and self-latching for safety.

WORKING WITH A PROFESSIONAL

THERE IS MUCH SATISFACTION to be had in pointing to a stunning poolside landscape and saying, "I did it all myself." The fact is, though, that even if you have the time, skill, and energy to do the job from start to finish, there are good reasons to enlist the help of professionals, especially during the design phase. Not the least of these reasons is that, while you may not be on top of all the breaking news, good landscape architects and designers have up-to-the-minute knowledge of changing building codes, safety regulations, materials, and technologies. Their savvy advice may lead you to creative options you didn't know existed—or save you from costly mistakes. But to get the most from your relationship with a pro, it pays to do a little homework first.

• Find your style. Peruse photographs in magazines and books. Go on local garden tours that include homes with pools. In each case, note which shapes, colors, plants, and materials appeal to you and why. Take photographs and clip articles. The more you can tell and show your future design helper about your likes, dislikes, and expectations, the more likely you'll be happy with the final result.

• Find your comfort range. Consider the complexity of your project, your level of experience, and the size of your budget—then decide how much you want to tackle. You may opt simply to get some basic design advice, then grab the ball and run with it. You may do the plant-related tasks yourself but rely on subcontractors for wiring, paving, and construction work. Or you may let pros do the job from start to finish.

• Find the right match. When it comes to a project as subjective as your own backyard, don't settle for the first name that leaps out from the phone book. When you're on a garden tour and find an appealing poolscape, ask who designed it. Solicit referrals from friends and neighbors. Other good sources of leads include nearby universities with landscape-architecture programs and the staffs of upscale nurseries and garden-accessory shops.

YOUR LANDSCAPE'S INFRASTRUCTURE

Once you've defined the broad goals for your landscape, take a good look at the elements within it. In one sense, your choices are governed only by your taste and budget, but in each case there are some practical guidelines to keep in mind.

WIRING   Nothing adds more to the allure of a pool or spa than good lighting. Fountains and other water features also demand wiring for electric pumps. Most likely some of your pool-related tasks will require the help of a pro, but it's easy to install low-voltage lighting yourself (see pages 180–181).

IRRIGATION   Depending on your plant choices and your climate, you may want to install a permanent irrigation system, either drip or sprinkler style, to make watering easier and more efficient. At the very least, make sure you have hose hookups in convenient locations.

DECKING   The surface around your pool or spa can range from a paved strip that's just wide enough for easy walking, to a series of interconnected patios and terraces made

OPPOSITE PAGE: This curved stairway leading down to the pool has built-in lights and a handrail, making it safe for people of all ages.

BELOW: Why limit yourself to one decking material when you can have three? This pool has wood on one side and, on the other, brick with a border of river rocks.

with anything from concrete pavers to handcrafted tile (see pages 146–149).

STAIRS AND PATHWAYS Spend some time pondering how you and your guests will move from house to pool to the broader landscape. Your options for surfacing paths and steps are even wider than they are for patios and decks.

WATER FEATURES Of course you can enjoy your daily dip without a waterfall or fountain, but these and other water features can add drama and elegance to your landscape. Although installation is best done while your pool is being built, it is possible to add many of these structures later. For a fountain that connects to your pool's return lines, you'll need a professional pool technician.

PUTTING YOUR PLAN ON PAPER

EVEN IF YOU INTEND TO hire a professional landscape architect or designer, it's a good idea to get your own ideas down on paper first. That task will be simpler if you use overlays, as described on page 46. This technique is especially helpful if you plan to complete your landscaping in phases, but it's also a great way to try out a variety of hardscape and planting schemes without having to redraw your entire plan each time. If you already have a plot plan that shows your pool or spa in place, that's your starting point. Otherwise, you'll need a large sheet of graph paper (ideally at least 16 by 20 inches) and sheets of tracing paper of the same size.

On the graph paper, draw your master plan—that is, your yard as it will be (or already is) with the pool or spa in place. Include your house and all plantings, hardscape, or structures that you regard as permanent. Also note the direction of prevailing winds, sources of unwanted noise, as well as views that you want to either block or emphasize. Be sure to indicate north on your plan so you'll know the path the sun will follow across the site.

To save space and avoid confusion, use symbols or colors to denote plants and other design elements, and make a master key that explains what each symbol means.

Tape a sheet of tracing paper over your master plan and sketch the additions you intend to make, such as a pathway and plantings. If you'll be completing your project over time, use a separate sheet for each phase of the work. To use this technique as a brainstorming method, simply make a different overlay for each set of variations you come up with.

surrounding
SURFACES

Strictly speaking, you don't need to have decking around your pool—a simple coping that caps its walls and joins it to the surrounding lawn works just fine. But smooth, flat, stable surfaces provide an added dimension to poolside life, giving you attractive, comfortable spaces for dining, entertaining, playing games, or just hanging out.

POOL DECKING

When it comes to pool decking, you have a multitude of materials to choose from. But the good ones all have several things in common.

FIRM, COMFORTABLE FOOTING It's important to remember that people who tread this surface will do so with bare, wet feet. Look for materials that reflect rather than absorb heat and that provide good traction without being coarse, uneven, or prone to splintering.

EASE OF MAINTENANCE Choose a surface that's easy to sweep or hose down—it will be the barrier between the pool and your landscape and will catch leaves, grass clippings, and all manner of other debris. Regardless of what it's made of, make sure the deck slopes away from the pool's coping by

¼ to ⅜ inch per foot. This will allow hose or rain water to drain away freely and will prevent water splashed out of the pool from flowing back in.

STAYING POWER Even more than most other outdoor surfaces, a pool deck takes a beating. Choose a material that will resist algae, bacteria, chemicals, frost, and fungi—not to mention your pets' occasional indiscretions—

as well as hard knocks from toppled furniture or mishandled lawn tools.

GOOD LOOKS It goes without saying that you want your deck to be attractive, but also keep in mind how it will blend with its surroundings. Seek out materials that complement the colors and textures of other paved areas as well as the architecture of your house.

OPPOSITE PAGE: A lush, green lawn is restful to the eye and welcoming to bare feet. But it does take a lot of water and maintenance.

ABOVE: If you're drawn to the look of a material that would be hard to walk on with bare feet, such as these irregular stones, you can make the decking around the pool a smooth surface and use the uneven material in an adjacent area.

CONCRETE

What was once considered gray and boring is now an art form in many installations. Concrete can be stamped to look like stone or brick, colored with pigments or stains, painted, or decorated with aggregates such as pebbles, marble, and glass. The possibilities are limited only by your imagination. Just make sure the surface isn't so smooth that wet feet will slip.

WOOD

If you want to build a poolside deck, you have several wood options. Pressure-treated wood is the least expensive. It turns a gray color if left unfinished, but you can also stain it any color. Redwood maintains rich wood tones if left unfinished; otherwise it will turn a silvery gray. The dark heartwood of redwood and

cedar is naturally resistant to rot. Western red cedar is the most abundant type, but in some areas you can find northern white, Alaska yellow, and others. The most expensive options are tropical hardwoods such as teak and mahogany. All wooden decks require seasonal maintenance, such as sanding and sealing to protect them from water damage and to keep them safe for bare feet.

ABOVE: Concrete decking works well in modern-style landscapes like this one. It's also durable, smooth, and relatively inexpensive.

LEFT: Wood decking is a beautiful choice. While natural wood needs resealing once a year, composite decking never needs to be resealed, is splinter-free, and looks similar to wood.

OPPOSITE PAGE, TOP: Irregular flagstone has a slightly textured surface with good traction.

OPPOSITE PAGE, BOTTOM: Brick decking has an elegant and traditional look, requires little maintenance, and can be laid in a variety of patterns.

COMPOSITES

Made from a combination of reclaimed wood and recycled plastic, composite decking has the appearance and workability of wood without many of its drawbacks. It doesn't splinter, it provides excellent traction even when wet, and it resists moisture, insects, and sunlight.

STONE

Precut stone tiles in square or rectangular shapes are fairly uniform in thickness and easy to lay in a grid pattern. Stubbed toes won't be as much of a problem as they might be with cleft stone, which has random widths and thicknesses. Slate is naturally water resistant, but pick a lighter shade so it stays cooler for bare feet. Flat flagstones blend well with plants and look

great with water features, but they can be hard to clean. River rocks work around a pool if installed properly, with the flat side up and the stones deeply embedded in mortar. Otherwise they will be too unstable to walk on with bare feet.

BRICK

Brick is weather resistant and long lasting, and it comes in colors such as burnt orange, pale yellow, dark brown, and red with white flecks. Outdoor bricks are graded according to their ability to withstand various types of weather. If you live where the ground freezes and thaws, choose common bricks rated SX. Make sure that moss doesn't grow on brick pool decking, as it can cause people to slip and fall.

STAIRS, PATHWAYS, AND PATIOS

The farther an area is from the water's edge, the more options you have in surface materials. Firm footing is still crucial, but skin-pleasing textures and temperatures are not. Therefore, you can freely use darker paving that might become too hot for bare feet, or wood decking that could deliver painful splinters. As with your pool deck, though, you will still want to consider texture and color, ease of maintenance, weather resistance, and drainage capability.

OPPOSITE PAGE, TOP: An old concrete slab was cut into pieces and used to build a retaining wall and stairs leading down to the spa.

BELOW: Instead of continuing the dark slate tiles on the patio down to the pool deck, the homeowners chose a light-colored scored concrete, which will stay cooler for bare feet on hot days.

LEFT: Meandering stairs made of natural stone blend into the surrounding landscape.

TIP

Reserve gravel, wood chips, and similar particles for paths, sitting areas, and planting beds that are far removed from the pool. Such small chunks migrate with amazing ease and can make pool maintenance a nightmare.

fences and
WALLS

A good fence or wall can be the hardest-working element in your landscape. Equipped with a secure gate, it helps ensure your privacy and peace of mind. But a fence or wall can also screen unwanted views, shield you from winds, provide vertical planting space, and much more.

PLAYING IT SAFE

Many towns and cities have regulations that specify the height of a fence surrounding a pool, the maximum size of any gaps within it, and whether or not the gate must have a self-closing mechanism. Laws regarding the extent of a fence also vary. Some communities require pools to be

ABOVE: This brick wall provides privacy and wind protection. Bamboo planted in a row in front of the wall has been pruned so that its leaves don't hide the stately brick.

LEFT: These stucco walls are interrupted by colorful panels of stacked terra-cotta roofing tiles. The spaces between the tiles let cool air filter through.

fenced on all four sides, while others need just the yard to be fenced—the house counts as the fourth side provided certain safety devices are installed on it. Before you begin the design process, check with your local authorities about relevant ordinances. Confer with your insurance agent too, as your liability policy may mandate precautions over and above those required by the building code. For more on pool and spa safety, including basic fencing guidelines, see pages 216–225.

REDUCING WIND

WHEN WIND IS A PROBLEM, the style of your fence can make a big difference. A solid fence provides little or no wind protection past the distance equal to its height (figure 1). To reduce wind flow, use fencing with openings at least $1/2$ inch but no more than 4 inches wide. Another possibility is to add a baffle to a solid fence to increase its wind-blocking ability.

To extend wind protection to a distance of approximately twice the height of the fence, angle a baffle 45 degrees into the wind (figure 2).

Eliminate the downward rush of wind by using a baffle angled 45 degrees with the wind. You'll feel warmest in the pocket below the baffle and at a distance equal to a little more than the fence height (figure 3).

CHOOSING A FENCE

You'll want a fence or wall that complements both your house and the other features in your landscape. However, that needn't limit your choice of materials or break your budget. Wood, iron, and aluminum can all form fences that range from rustic to grand. Even chain link and wire mesh can be disguised with vines, thick shrubs, or inexpensive facing panels. For fences that are close to the pool, use the most moisture-resistant materials you can find. Good choices include redwood or cedar heartwood, which naturally resist water; lumber made from recycled plastic; and rust-resistant, noncorrosive metals.

POOL SCREENS

When security is not a factor, an attractive screen can perform all the space-defining, environment-altering feats of a fence, often at a fraction of the cost. You might choose panels made from bamboo, reed, canvas, wood, safety glass, or translucent plastic; or plant a living screen of shrubs or trees. Either way, the result can be simple or elaborate, portable or stationary.

BUILDING A FREESTANDING SCREEN

This quick and easy privacy screen is composed of two lath grids in simple frames that are joined with hinges, but you can devise numerous variations on the theme.

This fence suits its rustic location and still meets safety requirements. The openings are too small for a child to fit through.

For instance, you can add more grids, sink the uprights into sand for portability, or fasten the grids to the back of a raised planting bed. Choose naturally decay-resistant wood, such as redwood or cedar heartwood, or, better yet, a lumber composite made from recycled plastic.

Build the lath grid before sizing the frame. Join the finished frames with three bifold hinges. To sink the posts in sand, dig three 2-foot-deep holes (the center hole needs to be wide enough to accommodate two 2 by 4s), pour 4 inches of sand in the bottom of each hole, and position the posts. Then fill the holes with more sand, packing it in firmly.

MATERIALS LIST
- Waterproof glue
- Nails or screws
- Three bifold hinges

FOR EACH GRID
- Six 1-by-2 uprights 5 feet long
- Nine 1-by-2 crosspieces 3½ feet long

FOR EACH FRAME
- Two 2-by-4 posts 7½ feet long
- One 2-by-4 crosspiece 3½ feet long

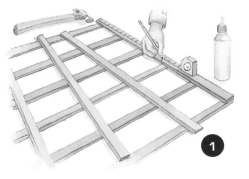

1 Lay the lath uprights facedown on a flat surface, then lay out the crosspieces. Space the pieces equidistantly, on approximately 8-inch centers, to make the grid. Place a dab of waterproof glue where the pieces cross. Then nail or screw each intersection. When the finished grid is flipped over, the fasteners will be out of sight.

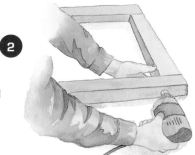

2 Size the frame pieces to fit around the finished grid, with the sides of the frame flanking the top piece. Use waterproof glue and countersunk screws to join the sides to the top.

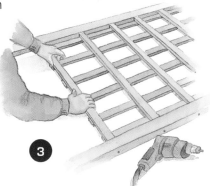

3 Slide the lath grid inside the frame. Drive in screws from the sides of the frame to keep the grid in place.

plants around
YOUR POOL

A central part of a successful landscape design is careful plant selection. Plants should suit your taste, complement your house and its surroundings, and thrive in the available growing conditions. When your landscape contains a swimming pool or spa, plant selection demands some additional considerations.

A POOL'S MICROCLIMATE

The area around a swimming pool is a harsh environment for plants. Chlorinated water and pool chemicals may be splashed on them, sometimes with fatal results. Strong sunlight, intensified by water and pavement, can burn delicate flowers and foliage. The pool itself, especially if it's heated, will raise the humidity in the immediate area, promoting mildew in susceptible plants. Finally, the first foot or so of ground next to a paved area—be it flowerbed or lawn—will probably receive more

RIGHT: Evenly spaced agaves in a raised planter are an excellent poolside choice, as they require little maintenance and can survive any reflected heat or chemical-laced splashes of water.

BELOW: Choose hardy plants if you want them to dip their leaves into a chemically treated pool.

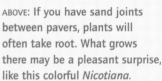

than its fair share of water from splashes and hosing off the deck. If all this makes you want to paint trompe l'oeil flowers everywhere, take heart. Plenty of beautiful plants are rugged enough to take just about everything your pool's microclimate can dish out.

To make wise choices, take notice of which plants grow well for your pool-owning neighbors. Chances are they'll perform like troupers in your yard, too. Gardening guides written for your area can also give you good insight into which plants will thrive.

ABOVE: If you have sand joints between pavers, plants will often take root. What grows there may be a pleasant surprise, like this colorful *Nicotiana*.

LEFT: Mixed ground covers provide color and texture unmatched by any solid decking material.

TIP

PLANTING

Plants that are classified as full-sun lovers may need some shade if they are subjected to the reflected light of a swimming pool.

PUTTING PLANTS TO WORK

No matter which part of your pool's surroundings you want to alter or improve, how and where you place your plants will make all the difference.

THE VIEW Hedges and trellised vines are classic choices for blocking an unpleasant view. But even strategically placed window boxes can shield you from a sight you'd rather leave unseen. When you've got the opposite challenge—a dramatic vista that you want to emphasize—a bold specimen plant or two can play the scene for all it's worth.

RIGHT: A vine climbing over a trellis provides some shade, while bright flowers and grasses add color to the woodsy landscape.

BELOW: Tall grasses create a private swimming oasis in a wide, open space.

The plants surrounding this pool were chosen to blend in with the stunning view.

WIDE-OPEN SPACES Whatever is on the agenda—from entertaining a crowd to curling up with a good book—plants can help you carve one large (or not-so-large) area into separate "rooms."

NOISE A dense hedge will help muffle sounds, but to really fight noise pollu-tion combine thick plantings with walls, fences, and fountains. (For more on water features, see pages 176–177.)

BRIGHTENING THE SCENE In a dim woodland setting, or for nighttime entertaining, use plants with white foliage and flowers. They'll sparkle among the trees and after dusk in a way that even pastel blooms can't match.

TIME

TIP
A swimming pool looks lovely sur-rounded by a lush, green lawn. But if that's the setting you choose, mow with care (or supervise your mowing crew) so that grass clip-pings don't wind up in the water.

HEDGE YOUR BETS

Whether you use them alone or in combination with walls and fences, hedges can perform a variety of tasks in your landscape, from guarding privacy to providing a dramatic backdrop for colorful flowers. Here are some tips to help you get the most from your green screen.

THINK AHEAD Purchase trees or shrubs that will be the size you need when they reach maturity. Don't be tempted by nursery

BELOW: A wall of green leaves pairs nicely with the bright reds, yellows, and blues in this courtyard, and it shrouds the spa area from view.

stock that's "just perfect" now. In a few years, those plants could grow into monsters that block your sun and take over your garden.

CONSULT CITY HALL BEFORE YOU PLANT Many communities have guidelines designed to protect solar access or beautiful views.

BEWARE OF SPEED DEMONS Before you zero in on fast-growing plants, consider two things. First, if you want to maintain a formal or semiformal style, rapid growers will demand almost constant clipping. Second, the trees and shrubs that grow quickly generally have shorter life spans than those with more moderate growth rates. If you're eager to achieve a lush, mature look right away, fill in with perennials for a few years.

THINK OUT AS WELL AS UP If your yard is small, a hedge might provide privacy but eat up half the available space. Maybe what you need isn't a hedge at all but a vine-covered trellis or a few trees espaliered against a wall or fence.

PLANTS TO KEEP AT A DISTANCE

How well your plants will grow is only one factor in their suitability for a poolside landscape. Their growth habits are also important —and become more so the closer they are to the water's edge. Here are some things to think about as you peruse catalogs or stroll down nursery aisles.

PROBLEM	SOME PRIME CULPRITS
Plant litter To avoid plant debris in the water, situate plants that drop leaves or flowers away from the pool. Likewise, keep plants that drop fruit or sap away from the pool deck as well as the water. Otherwise, you'll be asking for permanent stains, a slippery surface, and a lot of stinging insects flying in for sweet treats.	bougainvillea fruit trees and bushes (all) New Guinea impatiens willow *(Salix)* wisteria
Invasive roots Trees, shrubs, and rampant perennials that spread their roots far and wide can buckle your pavement and clog your water pipes. At best they'll make high-maintenance nuisances of themselves.	bamboo California fuchsia poplar *(Populus)* silver grass *(Miscanthus)* willow *(Salix)*
Mildew All the humidity around a pool can encourage mildew. Steer clear of plants that are prone to the disease.	asters bee balm *(Monarda)* black-eyed Susan *(Rudbeckia)* garden phlox *(Phlox paniculata)*
Bee attractants Yes, they add beauty and fragrance to your landscape. But they also attract bees, which you probably don't want joining the fun, so don't plant them right at the water's edge.	roses *(Rosa)* bee balm *(Monarda)* bottlebrush *(Callistemon)* borage buttonbush *(Cephalanthus occidentalis)* cosmos *(Cosmos bipinnatus)* honeysuckle *(Lonicera)* star jasmine *(Trachelospermum)*
Prickly or irritating plants Keep these far from the pool edge so people don't brush against them with bare legs.	barberry *(Berberis)* cacti pyracantha roses *(Rosa)* rue *(Ruta graveolens)*

GO FOR THE GREEN

You may want to eschew both decking and poolside planting beds in favor of a lush, green lawn. Few sights are lovelier or more relaxing than the cool interplay of blue water against green grass. And few surfaces are more welcoming to bare feet and wet bodies than a carpet of turf. If that's the setting you choose, keep these guidelines in mind.

LEAVE A BROAD BUFFER Installing an extra-wide coping around your pool will make mowing easier and help ensure that grass clippings don't wind up in the water.

BE PREPARED TO COMPROMISE The grasses that form the softest, most toe-tickling lawns perform best in cool weather, and they demand a lot of water. If your climate can't meet those standards, chances are you can still achieve your blanket of green by planting warm-season grasses or low-growing ground covers. But don't expect the same cushiony feeling you'd get from, say, Kentucky bluegrass.

BROADEN YOUR HORIZONS Instead of turf grass or as an accent to your lawn, consider planting ornamental grasses. They require little maintenance, they thrive in the harsh light and reflected heat from paved surfaces, and most varieties deposit little litter. In addition their soft, billowy textures provide a perfect complement to the flat smoothness of water—or close-clipped turf.

ESPALIERING

Training a tree or other plant to grow more or less flat against a wall or fence is a classic trick for saving space. It's also a great way to keep flowering or fruiting branches a safe distance from the water's edge.

MATERIALS LIST

- Trellis or wire
- Pruning shears
- Soft cloth or plastic ties

1 At planting time, choose two strong branches to form the tree's first tier; remove all other shoots and cut back the leader (the main trunk) to just above the bottom wire. Bend the branches at a 45-degree angle and secure them to the wire with soft cloth or plastic ties (not wire).

2 During the first growing season, continually and gradually tighten the ties so that by season's end the branches are horizontal. When the newly sprouted leader is long enough, hold it so it's erect and tie it to the second wire.

3 During the first dormant season, cut back the leader close to the second wire. Choose two branches for the second tier and prune off all competing shoots. Cut the lateral growth on the first-tier branches back to three buds.

4 During the second growing season, gradually bring the second-tier branches to a horizontal position, as described in step 2. Keep the leader upright and tie it to the third wire.

5 Repeat the process for a fourth wire if you have one. When the leader reaches the top wire, cut it back to just above the top branch. Keep horizontal branches in bounds by pruning back the ends to downward-facing side branches in the late spring and summer.

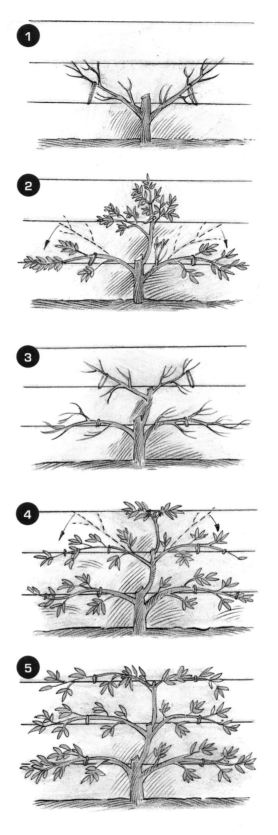

paradise
IN POTS

If your pool or spa and the surrounding pavement consume most of the space in your small yard, a container garden may be your only planting option. But even with acres of land at your disposal, you have plenty of good reasons to grow some plants in pots.

ARCHITECTURE ON THE GO

Because potted plants are portable, they make all but instant space dividers. You can gather them into an island bed, line them up to form a privacy hedge, or push them back against a wall when you need an open "party room."

A BROADER PALETTE

Containers let you indulge your taste for plants that wouldn't grow well—and might not even survive—in your setting. For instance, you can amend potting mix to suit any plant's requirements for texture, nutrients, or pH level. (In the ground, such soil-boosting measures will take you only so far.) You can whisk potted shade lovers to shelter when the sun gets too harsh, or move sun worshippers out of the shadows and into the light as necessary. Delicate specimens such as citrus trees, bougainvillea, passionflowers, and a multitude of tender herbs can sail through the summer on a northern patio, then spend the winter ensconced in a greenhouse or sunny window.

Xanthosoma 'Chartreuse Giant' planted in containers adds visual interest to the edge of a rectangular pool.

INSTANT GRATIFICATION

Watching your gardening efforts unfold each year at nature's pace can be both inspiring and gratifying. But there is also much to be said for buying pots of flowers in full bloom and setting them around the deck of your pool. With plants in containers, you also get to orchestrate the show from start to finish. For instance, when your spring tulips and daffodils pass their prime, you just move them out of the way and carry in replacements.

ABOVE: In small spaces, make your pots do double duty. The base of this one is filled with lava rock covered with bagged concrete mix. The umbrella fits into a plastic ABS pipe that was set in place before the concrete hardened. The top third of the pot was then filled with planting mix to accommodate some flowering plants. When you have no need for the umbrella, you can simply remove it and the plants will hide the pipe.

LEFT: On an existing paved patio, planting trees in the ground would be difficult. But with large pots, you can enjoy citrus trees and palms around the pool. The bases of the citrus pots are filled with rosemary, further scenting the air.

THE GREAT INDOORS

IN RECENT YEARS, the popularity of indoor pools and spas has grown by leaps and bounds, especially in northern climates, and the trend shows no sign of stopping. It's no wonder. Who wants to go to the trouble and expense of installing a pool that can be used only for a few months of the year? As practical as it may be, though, an indoor pool comes with a challenge: how to avoid the look and feel of a health club or chain hotel setting. The answer is container plants. They can help make your indoor space look like an outdoor paradise or a living room that just happens to contain a small body of water—the choice is yours. (Savvy furniture choices help too. For more on that, see pages 184–187.)

poolside
STRUCTURES

In one way, swimming pools and spas are like babies. In relation to their size, they seem to require an enormous amount of equipment, and new pool owners, like new parents, must find someplace to put it all. The obvious solution is a poolside building designed for the purpose.

There are plenty of other reasons for adding structures near your pool. For instance, you may want a covered space for entertaining, lounging, or even working on your laptop computer. Or perhaps you just want to protect your home's interior from all those wet towels and bathing suits. Whatever the size of your property or your budget, options abound for both specialized

and multipurpose structures. If installing your pool or spa puts a dent in your resources, erect the minimum shelter you need to protect your support equipment, then add more when you can.

This open-air pavilion is ideal for entertaining. On the left and right are bathrooms and storage for pool supplies. A second-story deck gives an even more impressive view of the pool and surrounding sculpture garden.

ABOVE: This stately pool house serves as a home office and provides a place for people to change and shower after using the pool.

TIP

TIME

To avoid unpleasant and possibly expensive surprises, check your town's zoning requirements before you build any pool structure, even if it's a prefab storage shed.

BELOW: Curtains around this covered porch can be pulled closed for quick swimsuit changes.

POOL HOUSES AND CHANGING ROOMS

The queen of water-side structures is the pool owner's version of a dream house: a full-blown pool house complete with wet bar, kitchen, bathroom, and maybe even a guest room. But just a shed big enough to allow a quick change of clothes will save you from a summer-long parade of people in wet bathing suits traipsing through your house. In the midrange there are myriad choices that give you sheltered space for entertaining, changing, and storage.

ARBORS AND PERGOLAS

These structures, which are designed to provide relief from the sun's heat, can be just large enough to shelter a table for two, spacious enough to cover a large deck, or any size in between. Regardless of size or style, an arbor or a pergola not only gives you a shady place to relax or party but can also solve the nagging problem of how to screen your site from above—for instance, to block the view from the windows of your neighbors' houses or a nearby apartment building.

RIGHT: Instead of the usual set of lounge chairs, this pergola surrounds a hammock, making it the perfect spot for an afternoon snooze by the pool.

BELOW: A climbing rose bush relies on this arbor for support and provides shade for afternoon tea.

BUILDING AN ARBOR OR A PERGOLA

The terms arbor and pergola are often used interchangeably, but there is a minor distinction between the two. Although both consist of posts supporting an open roof of beams or lattice, an arbor is broader and may be connected to a building on one side. A pergola, on the other hand, is always freestanding and narrow. Regardless of which of these shade-giving structures you choose to build, the technique is the same. This project is best done with two people. As for any permanent structure, consult your local building department before proceeding.

MATERIALS LIST

- 6-by-6 posts
- One post base and anchor bolt for each post (if you are affixing to concrete) or one precast concrete pier with post base, plus concrete mix (if you are building on soil)
- Galvanized nails
- One 1/2-by-10" lag bolt with washer per post
- Two 1/2-by-7" lag bolts with washers per beam
- Braces and wooden stakes
- Two 6-by-6 beams
- 4-by-4 rafters

1 Fasten each post base to the concrete with an anchor bolt (if building on the ground, dig a post hole, fill with concrete, and position the top of the precast pier 3 to 4 inches above grade level). Cut the posts to length if necessary. Nail the posts to the post bases.

2 Use a level on two adjacent sides to check that each post is vertical. Secure it in position with temporary braces nailed to wooden stakes that are driven into the ground.

3 With a helper, position a beam on top of the posts. Check that the posts are still vertical and the beam is level. Use a 7/16-inch bit to drill a 9-inch-deep hole down through the beam into each post. With a wrench, install a 10-inch lag bolt into the hole. Repeat for the other beam.

4 Set and space the rafters on top of the beams. With a 7/16-inch bit, drill 6-inch-deep holes through the rafters and into the beams. Install a 7-inch lag bolt into each hole. For more strength, you can install diagonal bracing between the posts and the beams. For shade, cover the rafters with vines or lath, either 1 by 2s or 2 by 2s.

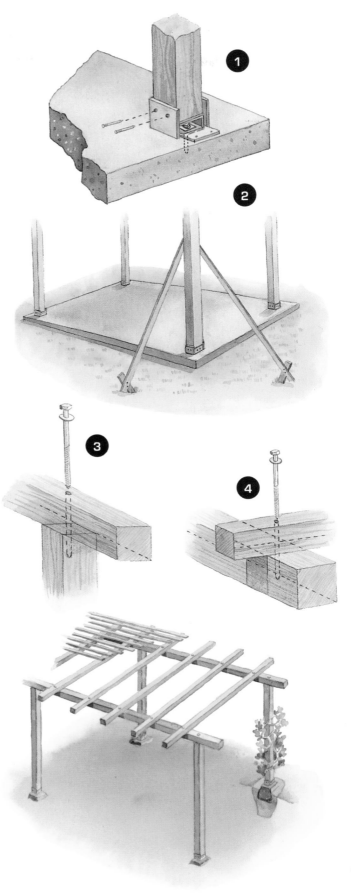

CABANAS AND GAZEBOS

Cabanas and gazebos are the landscaping equivalent to grandstands. They give you a sheltered place to sit and watch the action at poolside. Generally speaking, a cabana (the name comes from the Spanish word for "hut") has a solid roof, three lightweight walls, and one open side facing the object of your viewing pleasure—in this case, your pool. Gazebos have been standard features in English gardens since the 1600s and have gained widespread popularity in this country in the past decade or so. They are open on all sides, allowing people inside to sit and look across the landscape (the name may be a combination of the words "gaze" and "about").

SAUNAS

For increasing numbers of people, a sauna and a pool are a match made in heaven. Your sauna can be a freestanding structure, or it can be incorporated into a pool house,

ABOVE: A pool that's surrounded by a striking landscape deserves a classic gazebo. From this roofed but wide-open perch, no part of the scenery can escape the attention of admiring viewers.

BELOW: An updated take on a cabana, this structure has a solid roof but features curtains on the sides that can be closed to block sun and opened for a breeze.

garage, or basement. For more about saunas, including how to build your own, see pages 226–233.

STORAGE STRUCTURES

Although other pool-side structures are nice extras, sheltered storage space is a must. You'll need a fair amount of it for the vacuum, leaf skimmer, brushes, chemicals, and other pool equipment. Storing all those necessities in a covered, well-ventilated area will not only keep them out of sight but also prolong their life. Most likely you will also need room to store outdoor furniture, play and fitness gear, and other accessories when they're not in use.

A shed that you put together from a kit is a fast, easy, and inexpensive answer to the question "Where can we put all this stuff?!" There's just one drawback: Fresh out of the box, a prefab storage shed has about as much visual pizzazz as the box it came in. Fortunately, with a little imagination and a few simple tools, you can solve that problem in a few hours.

Painted to match your house and decorated with gingerbread from an architectural salvage dealer—or reproduction trim from your local lumberyard—a bland shed becomes a charming Victorian outbuilding.

Trompe l'oeil paintings on the door panels, a wooden heart above the frame, and a flower box beneath a framed-mirror "window" say, "Make mine country style."

If yours is an Asian-inspired landscape, adorn your shed with willow or bamboo panels and surround it with rock constructions, stone lanterns, and bamboo and stone fountains.

sun
PROTECTION

Swimming pools and spas invite you to spend more time outdoors, which is a good thing as long as you protect yourself from the sun.

SHADE SAILS

These taut fabric canopies are stretched from three or more points, and they often look like the sail of a ship. Choose a sail made of high-tech fabric that blocks ultraviolet rays. When you have a large area to cover, shade sails are more economical than multiple umbrellas or retractable awnings. They also have a unique look and can add style and dimension to an otherwise vanilla landscape.

UMBRELLAS

Umbrellas can be found in a rainbow of colors and patterns. Heavy bases that you can lift or turn on their side and roll are often sold separately. It's easier to move the base where you want it and then set the umbrella's pole into the base. If you

BELOW LEFT: Ready-made sails put the shade where you want it and are easy to maintain. Just hose them off when they get dirty.

BELOW RIGHT: Swaths of retractable fabric run across the side of this pool, providing all-day shade.

branches were laid overhead for shade. Today, any open-air structure with some form of sun protection on top—free-standing or attached to a house—can be called a ramada. Fashion your own out of any material, be it stone columns or metal posts, with canvas or woven matting on top. Add lighting for when the sun goes down and you'll have a multi-purpose space for relaxing outdoors.

LEFT: Portable umbrellas can be moved from one seat to the next as the sunlight shifts during the day.

BELOW: This ramada has a bamboo roof, which protects more delicate furniture and light fixtures from sun and rain.

want to leave the umbrella up most of the time, buy a high-quality model that resists fading and mildew. Less expensive umbrellas are often lighter and will last longer if you store them in the garage. Look for outdoor tables that will take an umbrella pole so you can enjoy some shade while you're eating.

RETRACTABLES

Using any type of outdoor fabric, you can create a retractable shade just by installing rows of wire across an area, sewing grommets into the edges of the fabric, and then pulling the fabric across the wire with the end of your pool skimmer. Choose fabric with an ultraviolet rating for the best sun protection.

RAMADAS

Classic ramadas were made with four tree trunks set into the ground in a square. Horizontal pieces of wood across the tops connected the four trunks, and then

outdoor SHOWERS

One way to keep your pool clean is to make sure only clean bodies swim in it. An outdoor shower will allow people to rinse off quickly before diving in. It also comes in handy for rinsing pool chemicals off your skin and hair after a dip.

LOCATION

The least expensive way to construct an outdoor shower is to tap into an existing water source. If the nearest water comes from an outdoor spigot used for landscape irrigation, you'll be able to take only cold showers. Find where the hot and cold water supply pipes enter your house and see if you can place your outdoor shower nearby. Another option is to build the outdoor shower on the opposite wall of an indoor bathroom that has water supply pipes running inside the exterior wall. If necessary, you can trench from the hot and cold water supply pipes over to where you want the shower, then have a plumber run new pipes underground to that location.

If you think you'll use your outdoor shower for soaping and shampooing after a swim, you might want to put it in a private area where bathing suits are optional. You can also create privacy with plantings, panels, or curtains.

MATERIALS

An outdoor shower can be as plain or as fancy as you want it to be. Shop at building salvage stores to find unique

This shady side yard has two water features: a fountain and a shower. Plumbing is built into a freestanding tiled wall, and the fountain sits on a concrete base so it can be seen from indoors.

plumbing fixtures and leave the hardware exposed for a rustic look. You can also hide the pipes inside a wall or post and have the showerhead and handles

LEFT: An upscale outdoor shower features the same materials and fixtures you'd find in an indoor bathroom.

RIGHT: If your shower lacks privacy, add a couple of posts and a gate in lieu of a door. Here, a shrub acts as a fourth wall.

BELOW: A shade- and water-loving vine climbs the wall of this chic and private shower.

exposed, just as in an indoor shower. Consider installing a handheld shower-head if you will be rinsing small children.

DRAINAGE

The shower water needs to go some-where. It will involve some trenching, but you can have a plumber create a drain that ties into your home's sewer line. Another option is to build a dry well for the water to drain into. Make your own dry well by digging a round hole about 4 feet deep. Find a plastic container that will fit inside the hole, then drill holes all the way around it. Line the hole with landscape cloth and then place the container inside the hole. Backfill the hole with soil and fit a removable drain over the top of the con-tainer. Water from the shower will slowly absorb into the surrounding soil. Check the container every so often to make sure it's not filling up with silt. The landscape cloth will help keep the container clean.

water on
WATER

The sight, sound, and feel of moving water can relax our bodies, inspire our minds, and restore our spirits. As with all the other elements in your landscape, you will want to select water features that complement the style of your pool and its surroundings, and suit your taste, budget, and the way you use your pool.

WATERFALLS

Whether you have a waterfall installed at the time your pool is built or add one later, you have an enormous range of styles and effects from which to choose. You can simulate the look and sound of the real thing, with water cascading over time-worn boulders, either real or synthetic. Or you can abandon all pretense in favor of a simple sheet of water flowing over marble, stone, or concrete.

FOUNTAINS

Of all water features, a fountain is the easiest to add, because you already have the essentials in place: pumps and access to the electricity powering the pool equipment. You can buy ready-made fountains in nurseries, garden shops, and home centers; seek out a handmade original in craft galleries; or make your own. Anything that spouts water will do the job, from an antique urn to a rock with a hole drilled in it. Whichever spouting device you choose, though, fountains

A rushing waterfall makes this man-made swimming pool seem like something that nature built.

that function in conjunction with swimming pools fall into three basic categories: fountainheads installed inside the pool, fixtures that sit on or under the coping and shoot water into the pool, and wall-mounted fountains that spill into the pool. All are best installed when the pool is constructed but can be added later. In almost every case you'll need the help of a professional pool technician. If you want to simply enjoy the sight and sound of moving water, you can easily make a free-standing or wall-mounted self-contained fountain.

RIGHT: A wide waterfall can catch the eye of people inside the house, and its sound can block traffic noise if you live on a busy street.

BELOW LEFT: The higher the fountain, the louder the sound of splashing water.

BELOW RIGHT: Water falls from this copper urn into the pool below. It looks like the water comes from the bog garden behind it, but pool water is recirculated up through the stone wall.

the pool
BY NIGHT

If you take nocturnal dips or throw frequent evening pool parties, the illumination of your pool is a major aesthetic consideration. Good lighting is also a must from a safety standpoint. Check with your town's building department and your insurance company about guidelines that may mandate certain types or levels of lighting.

LIVING IN THE LIGHT

Good outdoor lighting is both functional and aesthetically pleasing. On the practical side, it offers the right kind of light when and where you need it for entertaining, al fresco cooking or dining, or just relaxing. At the same time, judicious lighting adds to the aura of your pool or spa by highlighting architectural features and plantings or by casting a magical glow on the water—viewed from indoors or out.

LEFT: If you don't want to incorporate electric lights into your pool, you can always brighten the path to it with candle-powered tiki torches.

OPPOSITE PAGE: This pool provides entertainment well into the night with fountains and a soft lighting design.

BELOW: A soft green glow allows you to see the pool without lighting up the entire yard, which may annoy neighbors.

TIP

DESIGN

Not sure where you need light? Experiment with inexpensive clip-on lamps that you can buy at your local hardware store. Just plug them into outdoor-grade extension cords and fasten them to tree limbs or fences, or ask a helper to hold them aloft as you ponder the placement possibilities.

STREETLIGHT-STYLE PATH LIGHT

LIGHTING OPTIONS

A traditional 120-volt outdoor lighting system requires buried, waterproof pipes that meet local safety codes. That can translate into a long wait for a busy electrician, followed by a large bill for services. Fortunately, you have a faster and far less expensive option: low-voltage outdoor lighting, which uses only 12 volts of electricity. The easy part is installing a transformer that steps down the voltage from 120 to 12. The hard part is deciding where you want to place your lights, the kind of effect you want to achieve, and which of the multitude of available fixtures you want to use.

INSTALLING LOW-VOLTAGE LIGHTS

Building-supply stores sell attractive low-voltage lighting kits that are a snap to install. You'll need to plug the transformer into a properly installed GFCI-protected outdoor outlet; if you don't have one, a professional electrician can easily install it. Lay out the wire in a direct route, following the manufacturer's directions. Don't let the wire cross over itself, and avoid tight, twisty turns. Be sure not to add more lights than the kit's maker prescribes.

SOLAR LIGHT WITH INSTALLATION HARDWARE

MATERIALS LIST

- Low-voltage lighting kit
- Tape measure
- Pliers
- Insulated screwdriver
- Wire cutter with stripper
- Shovel
- Twine, garden hose, lime, or flour (for marking route)

THREE-TIERED PATH LIGHT

LOW-PROFILE FLOODLIGHT

POST CAP LIGHT

1 Lay out the route you want your lights to illuminate. You can snake twine or a garden hose on the ground, or simply sprinkle lime or white flour along the desired path. Then dig a trench at least 6 inches deep following the outline.

2 Position the light fixtures along the route beside the trench. Lay the low-voltage cable in the trench and clip the wire leads extending from each light fixture to the cable. Some types of lights screw to the cable rather than clip.

3 Drive the attached ground spikes into the soil. Cover the cable with mulch or soil.

4 Near the GFCI receptacle and in a spot not likely to be bumped, mount the transformer with screws drilled into a stable surface. Following the manufacturer's directions, connect the wires to the transformer, using an insulated screwdriver.

5 Plug the transformer into a GFCI-protected outlet. Adjust the settings to turn the lights on and off automatically at particular times of day.

adding FIRE

Having a heat source near the pool can make drying off after a cold-weather dip more enjoyable, or a summer night party more festive. Some communities have outlawed wood-burning fireplaces for environmental reasons, so check with your local building office before installing one.

FIREPLACES

A wood-burning masonry fireplace blends with nature and gives you that campfire smell. But the footings, fire-brick-lined firebox, and chimney can make this an expensive proposition. If you can build the outdoor fireplace up against a house wall that has an existing chimney, you can avoid the expense. Be sure to site the fireplace away from adjacent homes and low-hanging trees. The chimney should have a spark arrester for safety.

ABOVE: For portable warmth and inexpensive charm, a chiminea is hard to beat.

OPPOSITE PAGE, LEFT: Poolside evening meals are more enjoyable when you're sitting by a fire.

BELOW: This cozy fire pit is just steps from the spa. A concrete bench is covered with cushions and pillows that can be stored indoors during the off-season.

Prefabricated gas-fired or wood-burning fireplaces have fireboxes made of stainless steel and metal chimneys. Some gas models are front vented and the exhaust is released through slots in the face frame, so you don't need a chimney. The units can be framed with wood or metal studs, encased in plywood, and finished with stucco, stone, or tile.

FIRE PITS

These low structures can burn wood or gas. The pit can be made with many materials, including brick, stone, and stucco. Build a square or circular pit near the spa, in the middle of a seating area. Make sure you can reach it with a stick while seated for roasting marshmallows. The fire pit itself can also have a built-in seat around the edge, as the flames usually stay low and in the center of the structure.

CHIMINEAS

If a fireplace or fire pit is too permanent or expensive a structure, there is another safe way to enjoy an outdoor fire. Chimineas are three-legged clay pots that look like old Mexican bread ovens. You can often find various styles at pottery stores. Relatively lightweight, they are easy to move around the yard, depending on where you want the warmth of a fire. Be sure to add a spark screen and a heatproof mat if you use it on a wooden deck.

HEAT LAMPS

For outdoor warmth without the risk of open flames, consider a stand-up portable patio heater. These typically run on propane and have a reflector on top that disperses warmth over a large area. For an electric solution, try an infrared heater installed overhead and pointed at the space you want to warm up. Most run on a standard 120 volts.

ABOVE: **This popular propane patio heater looks like a floor lamp and generates a warm red glow of infrared heat at the top, fueled by the propane tank at the base.**

the finishing
TOUCHES

In the past few decades, open-air living has become a national pastime—even if, in many places, it's possible for only two or three months of the year. When you are choosing furniture and accessories for your pool or spa setting, the choices can be mind-boggling, but they needn't be.

FURNITURE SHOPPING

Regardless of whether you need enough furniture to accommodate several dozen partygoers or just a table and chairs for two, there are four considerations worth bearing in mind: style, size, durability, and—most important of all—comfort. Before you purchase any furniture, try it out. Recline in the lounge chairs, pull the dining chairs up to the table, settle into the easy chairs, and put your feet up on the ottomans. If the people in your household vary greatly in stature, have them "test drive" the pieces too. It's rare that one size fits all, so you may want to buy chairs or benches in several different sizes, even if they don't exactly match.

QUALITY While it's tempting to buy the least expensive outdoor furniture you can find, consider the longevity of a piece before making your decision. If you buy something that isn't well made and doesn't have the kind of finish or fabric that will withstand the elements, chances are you'll have to get rid of it in a few years. It's better to buy high-quality outdoor furniture from the start.

Choose wooden furniture that's harvested from sustainable forests and constructed with mortise-and-tenon joinery and marine-quality hardware. The look of wicker is a popular out-door choice, but traditional wicker can break down outdoors over time. Many companies now sell furniture that looks just like wicker but is made of weatherproof resin strands that resist fading, cracking, and tearing. If you prefer metal chairs and tables, buy rustproof metals that have been coated to resist damage from ultraviolet light.

Metal furniture can be heavy, which is one sign of high quality, so look for pieces that include glides on the bottom so you won't scratch up your decking when scooting closer to the table.

CUSHIONS   It used to be that you'd have to take outdoor cushions inside every night lest they get moldy, or you'd settle for a rough woven fabric. But now there are comfortable outdoor cushions available in a range of hip colors and patterns, made of fabrics that resist fading, stains, and mildew.

OPPOSITE PAGE: Metal chairs with taut outdoor fabric can be left outside year-round and hosed off before use. Add a throw pillow for more cushioning.

RIGHT: Wooden furniture looks beautiful and natural outdoors, but it should be kept sealed to protect it from the elements.

BELOW: High-quality resin furniture that looks like wicker holds up well outdoors. Under a cabana, the pillows and cushions are protected from rain.

TIP

SMART Protect your outdoor furniture with waterproof covers. Some will endure subzero weather, and the best ones have vents to allow air circulation and ties that secure them to the furniture.

ACCESSORIES

In your poolscape, accessories function just as they do inside your home. They help you turn a pleasant but bland space into one that says, "This is mine!" There are no rules for choosing poolside decor, but bear in mind that more is not better. Too many objects near the pool can pose dangers to people moving about the deck. One or two outstanding pieces, placed at a safe distance from the water, will add visual pizzazz without putting swimmers at risk. If space is tight, look for objects that are useful as well as decorative—for instance, a quirky folk art sculpture that can double as a towel rack, a bench that's also a work of art, or a one-of-a-kind planter.

ABOVE: Mix store-bought furniture with antiques and pieces you make yourself. A side table like this can be found at a flea market and spruced up with a new mosaic tile top. It looks great next to a cushioned lounge chair.

LEFT: Old metal chairs painted in bright colors are low-maintenance outdoor furniture options.

OPPOSITE PAGE, TOP: This Moroccan-style backyard takes lying by the pool to a whole new level. An antique wrought-iron bed frame and a futon frame are topped with custom-made upholstered mattresses. Gold embroidery and tassels on the umbrellas add to the magical feel.

OPPOSITE PAGE, BOTTOM: A hammock is less expensive than most outdoor furniture but is just as comfortable for napping.

party
TIME

Dressing up your backyard for a pool party is one of the pleasures of owning a pool. Having that beautiful expanse of blue water makes any event feel more festive.

DAILY GATHERINGS

Many families use the pool and surrounding yard more than their living rooms, especially if the space includes places to sit and relax, eat, and cook. Imagine grilling hamburgers or tofu burgers in an outdoor kitchen on summer nights while the kids burn off their energy playing in the pool. It could be a simple portable grill with a side table for prep work and supplies. Or you may choose to build a fully equipped outdoor kitchen with a sink, lots of counter

ABOVE: To block the sun during midday parties, lengths of billowy fabric are pulled across on wires overhead. Guests can choose to eat on the cushioned banquette or at the bar.

BELOW LEFT: Ideal for entertaining, this backyard includes areas to swim, play, rest, and eat. The outdoor kitchen faces the pool so parents can keep an eye on swimming kids. A mirror along the back wall (see photo above) ensures children are never out of sight.

BELOW RIGHT: This candlelit indoor-outdoor space is an elegant spot to enjoy after-dinner drinks.

space, and even an outdoor refrigerator (see Sunset's *Barbecues & Outdoor Kitchens* for more information). Either way, be sure to situate it in a spot where you can keep an eye on the pool activity.

Provide lots of small seating areas so that adults or teenagers can read or do homework outside while younger children play in the pool. It's also crucial to set up some sort of sun protection if you plan to spend most days enjoying your backyard. Choices range from portable umbrellas and shade sails to structures such as gazebos and trellises (see pages 166–173).

FAMILY EVENTS AND BIRTHDAYS

Special occasions like birthdays and Sunday brunch with the in-laws may call for a bit more formality than your average weeknight barbecue. For these events, you might break out the tablecloths and china. Indoor accessories like these, or teacups and crystal candlesticks, make an outdoor party feel special. Round out the table with fresh-cut flowers from the garden and cloth napkins.

If your pool has a water feature, you can enjoy the sound of rushing water along with your outdoor meal. With a little more effort, you can dress up the pool itself. Large flowers look beautiful floating across the water. You can also find floating cups to hold up small candles. For an adult birthday party, the guest of honor may appreciate her age represented in the number of candles floating on the water rather than stuck on the cake.

Perched high above the pool is a lovely spot for brunch. The eating area is protected from the weather, and the drapes can be drawn for sun or wind protection.

LARGE PARTIES

With a beautiful pool and a large back-yard, you'll get year-round requests to hold everything from office parties to graduation events at your house. Get creative with your decorating to take things up a notch. Consider hosting a theme party. Offer grass skirts and leis to your guests, and then float a couple of surfboards in the pool and hang paper lanterns from a pergola. Or set up outdoor tents with piles of throw pillows and candles on tall pedestals for an exotic look. Stretch rows of white lights across the pool for a night party. The lights will reflect in the water and look like a meteor shower.

OPPOSITE PAGE, TOP: For people who don't like to swim, it's great to offer another outdoor activity to keep the party going. This bocce court provides hours of fun for guests of all ages, and it's close enough for adults to keep watch over the pool area.

OPPOSITE PAGE, BOTTOM LEFT: Colorful lanterns create a festive poolside atmosphere.

OPPOSITE PAGE, BOTTOM RIGHT: Take a cue from hotel pools and spas and provide rolled white towels in baskets for guests. When the sun goes down, these lanterns can be placed on tables throughout the pool area.

ABOVE: Provide several small seating areas rather than one large one so that smaller groups can gather for more intimate conversations.

RIGHT: The bright colors, funky furniture, and retro fire pit make this pool area perfect for a teenage party.

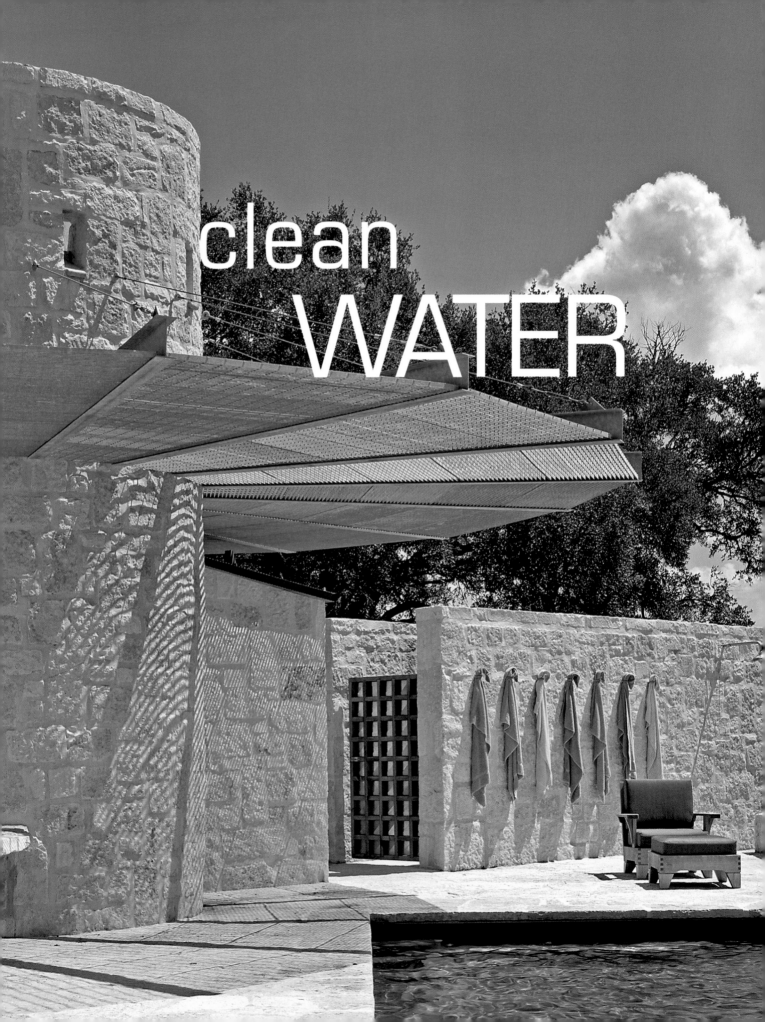

clean
WATER

WHEN IT COMES TO maintaining pristine water,
the filtration system and pump do the bulk
of the work. But periodic sanitizing, along
with adjustment of the water's chemical
balance, is also necessary to keep the
pool or spa free of contaminants and
comfortable for swimmers.

sanitizing
THE WATER

Disease-carrying microorganisms and algae thrive in water—particularly in the heated water of spas—so regular sanitizing is essential. Techniques range from the traditional practice of adding chlorine, to newer technology that requires almost no chemicals to do the job.

HOW CHLORINATION WORKS

Chlorine is the most popular choice for controlling pathogens in pool water. Not only does it kill algae and bacteria, it also breaks down organic debris by oxidizing it. Chlorine is available in three forms: liquid, which is rarely used for residential pools; granular, which is dissolved in water before being added; and slow-dissolving tablets, which are placed in a floating feeder that gradually releases chlorine into the water.

No matter which form you use, the chlorine reacts with your pool or spa water to produce, among other substances, hypochlorous acid. This com-pound, also referred to as free chlorine, is what actually does the sanitizing. However, hypochlorous acid degrades fairly quickly when exposed to sunlight. To counteract this, a stabilizing agent, most often cyanuric acid, is typically added to the water along with chlorine.

To determine whether your water needs chlorination, test the chlorine level a few times a week using a test kit from a pool-supply store. (Buy a kit that also measures pH level, total alkalinity, and calcium hardness, all

Clear water looks deceptively natural, but maintaining it is the result of careful chemistry.

discussed on the following pages.) The amount of free chlorine should be 1.0 to 2.0 parts per million (ppm).

The exact amount of chlorine to add to your pool depends on multiple factors, including the brand and how heavily your pool is used. In general, expect your pool or spa to need a daily dose of chlorine during periods of heavy use. Be sure to follow the package directions carefully.

CHLORINE'S SHORTCOMINGS

As hypochlorous acid encounters ammonia or nitrogen in the water—introduced by swimmers in the form of perspiration, saliva, and urine—it oxidizes those compounds, leaving behind chloramines. Chloramines have little capacity to further sanitize the water, and they can actually be an irritant. When a pool has a strong "chlorine" smell or stings swimmers' eyes, it's usually a sign of too little free chlorine. The cure is superchlorination, also known as a shock treatment—a high dose of chlorine added to the water to break down chloramines. You'll know it's time to superchlorinate when a strong smell becomes evident, or when ordinary chlorination does not clear the water.

SHOCKING THE POOL

A shock treatment is something you can administer on your own, using a chemical shocker (also called an oxidizer or

ADDING CHEMICALS SAFELY

POOL CHEMICALS CAN be extremely corrosive, posing a threat not only to the lining of the pool or spa but to the person adding them. In most cases, you will need to add chemicals manually and therefore, very carefully. Be sure to protect your eyes and hands.

To add granular chemicals, mix them first in a bucket by adding the granules to the water; never pour water on top of granules, because they are likely to splash out and can cause serious injury. Add the resulting liquid to the pool at various points, pouring close to the surface to minimize splashing. Add liquid chemicals the same way. To add large tablets, simply place them in a feeder.

burner). It usually comes in the form of a powder that is sprinkled into the water. You'll typically need to shock the pool about once a week during the swimming season and more frequently if the pool is used heavily.

Different shockers release different amounts of available chlorine to do the job, so check the instructions on the package. Also make sure the pump and filter are turned on. Keep everyone out of the pool for several hours after a shock treatment; it takes that long for the chlorine level to return to normal.

THE SALT ADVANTAGE

The chemicals that are used to chlorinate a pool or spa warrant careful handling, as they can be extremely hazardous. One recent advance eliminates that danger by deriving chlorine from ordinary table salt,

sodium chloride, that's periodically added to the pool water. The device, a chlorine generator, creates an electric current that splits salt molecules and releases chloride ions into the water.

Chlorine generators can be used for large in-ground pools, as well as above-ground pools and spas. The amount of salt required will depend on the size and location of your pool and the specific chlorine generator. But even when a seemingly large amount of salt is needed, it's relatively low compared with the salt in seawater, which means the water won't taste salty.

Instead of adding pure chlorine to the water, you can sanitize your pool in creative ways. A chlorine generator (above), releases chlorine when ordinary salt is added to the water. A floating ionizer (below) uses a solar-generated electrical current to release small amounts of algae- and bacteria-fighting minerals.

A pool or spa with a chlorine generator will still need periodic shocking with high levels of chlorine to keep the water clear. Some types of chlorine generators have a large enough capacity to produce these high levels themselves. A dial is simply set to "shock," and the generator does the work. Others, though, are not large enough to handle this task and require chlorine to be added separately when the level of chloramines is too high. (The addition of chlorine to the pool or spa will not interfere with the production of chlorine by the generator.)

THE BROMINE ALTERNATIVE

Chemically similar to chlorine, bromine has become a popular alternative for sanitizing indoor pools and spas. (It's not a viable option for outdoor pools because it breaks down quickly in the presence of sunlight.) Bromine kills pathogens via oxidation, the same way that chlorine does. However, bromine combines with organic matter to form bromamines rather than chloramines; bromamines do not produce the same acrid smell that chloramines do and are less noxious to the eyes and skin. Bromamines break down by natural processes, so there is no need to perform shock treatment.

SOLAR IONIZATION

One method of water purification that is gaining popularity is solar ionization. Borrowing a technique from ancient Rome, where metal coins were used to keep water fresh, a solar ionizer releases trace amounts of copper and silver into

TESTING AND ADJUSTING It's simple to measure your water's pH using a test kit from a pool-supply store. Special paper strips change color when you dampen them with a drop of pool or spa water. Matching the strips against a color chart yields a reading.

If the reading lies outside the optimum range, you will need to adjust the pH by adding either an acidic or an alkaline substance. For a pH below 7.2, add sodium carbonate, known as soda ash, or sodium bicarbonate, which is ordinary baking soda. If the pH is above 7.8, add muriatic acid or sodium bisulfate to lower it. The exact amount of treatment to add and the method for adding it will vary, so check labels.

TOTAL ALKALINITY

Although this component of water chemistry is closely related to pH, the two are subtly—and importantly—different. Total alkalinity (TA) is a measure of the quantity of alkaline material in water, regardless of whether

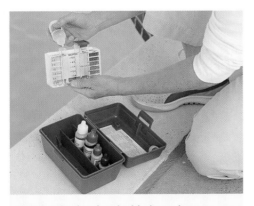

Maintain the chemical balance in your pool to protect the investment of building it, and to make it more enjoyable to use.

HOW OFTEN TO TEST

MEASUREMENT	POOL	STAND-ALONE SPA
Free chlorine	Once or twice a week	Twice a week
pH	Once a week	Twice a week
Total alkalinity	Once a week	Twice a week
Calcium hardness	At the start of the season	Once after each filling
Total dissolved solids	At the start of the season	Every two to three months, depending on use

it's balanced by an equal quantity of acidic material. Therefore, two samples of water that have a pH of 7.2 can differ in their total TA.

The ideal TA is between 80 and 150 parts per million (ppm), depending on the type of pool. For plaster-coated gunite pools the number should tend toward the low end of the spectrum, from 80 to 125 ppm; for vinyl, fiberglass, and painted-plaster surfaces it should tend toward the upper end, from 125 to 150 ppm. A TA that's too low can lead to rapid fluctuations in the water's pH, sometimes described as the water having no buffering capability. A TA that's too high makes it difficult to correct or adjust the pH—the water is too buffered. It's important to have the right amount of buffering in your pool so you can adjust the pH as well as avoid rapid fluctuations.

A test kit contains stoppered bottles for collecting water samples, along with tablets to dissolve in the water. The number of tablets required to change the water from yellow to pink indicates

TIP

COST

When you are adding chemicals —whether to increase the chlorine level or to adjust the pH—it's best to add a little at a time and check the effect, especially with spas, where only a small amount of chemicals can change the balance. Proceeding cautiously will save chemicals as well as money. You can always add more if necessary.

the total alkalinity in parts per million. To guarantee proper readings, it's essential to keep the sample vials clean and free of contamination. Plunge a test vial under the water with the cap on. Remove the cap, fill the vial with water, then screw the cap back in place underwater. This ensures that the sample isn't affected by debris floating on the surface. Above all, do not cover the opening of the vial with your finger; instead, use the cap. Oils and acids from your skin can alter the results.

If the TA is too high, you can lower it with muriatic acid; if it's too low, use sodium bicarbonate—baking soda—or chemicals found in pool-supply stores.

To determine how much muriatic acid to add, you'll first need to know your pool's volume (see page 91). Divide the volume in gallons by 125,000, then multiply by the number of parts per million change desired. This provides the amount of muriatic acid in quarts. If, for instance, your pool holds 10,000 gallons, and you want to decrease total alkalinity by 20 ppm, you would need to add 1.6 quarts of muriatic acid (10,000 ÷ 125,000 = .08 quarts for each ppm decrease; × 20 for 20 ppm = 1.6).

To determine how much sodium bicarbonate to add, the rule is that each increase of 10 ppm requires .14 pounds of bicarbonate for every 1,000 gallons. To raise the alkalinity 20 ppm in a 10,000-gallon pool, for example, you would add 2.80 pounds of sodium bicarbonate (.14 × 10 = 1.40 pounds for each 10 ppm increase; × 2 for 20 ppm = 2.80 pounds).

CALCIUM HARDNESS

Water is often described as hard or soft. The terms refer to the amount of dissolved minerals it contains. Hard water contains more minerals—of which calcium is the most common—while soft water contains less.

Where pools and spas are concerned, water that is too hard can turn cloudy, have an elevated pH, and cause calcium scales to form. (High water temperatures also encourage scaling.) Water that's too soft can soften or etch plaster, causing tile grout to dissolve and tiles to pop off, and create cracks in vinyl liners. Not all test kits measure calcium levels, although the more sophisticated ones do. If yours doesn't, you can take a sample of water to a pool store for testing.

In most cases, the calcium ion content of water should be maintained between 200 and 400 ppm. To increase the water's hardness— that is, to add more calcium ions—mix the chemical chloride dihydrate into the water at a rate of .1 pound for every 2,500 gallons. Decreasing hardness is more difficult. The most effective way is to drain some of the water from the pool and dilute what remains with softer water. A professional can also filter the calcium ions from the water with a nano-filter, which can remove the most minute particles imaginable. Another, less effective way to lower calcium levels is to add sodium hexametaphosphate, which causes the calcium to react and form particles that can be trapped by the pool's filtration system.

TOTAL DISSOLVED SOLIDS

Total dissolved solids, or TDS, is a measure of everything dissolved in water, including chemicals, minerals, residue from bathers (such as sunscreen), and all other impurities. These inert substances become more concentrated as water evaporates, resulting, over time, in cloudy water. The accumulation of TDS also causes sanitizers to become less effective, increasing the likelihood of algae growth, scaling, staining, and corrosion.

A TDS meter lets you monitor the level easily. You can also take a sample of water to a pool store to have it measured. To avoid elevated TDS levels (higher than 2,500 ppm), you can regularly add alum-based clarifiers, such as aluminum sulphate or sodium bisulphate (also known as dry acid), to your pool or spa. An even better approach is to periodically drain the pool a few inches and add fresh water.

If the TDS density reaches 2,500 ppm, more drastic action needs to be taken.

Drain the pool or spa completely, then refill it with fresh water. In a heavily used swimming pool, you might have to do this every three or four years. By contrast, a 300-gallon spa used by two people per day would reach TDS overload in just 50 days of use.

OVERALL BALANCE

Even if pH, TA, calcium hardness, and TDS all fall within recommended limits, the water in a pool or spa may still cause scaling or corrosion. If this is the case, it may help to have a pool professional consult an overall indicator of water balance known as the Langelier Saturation Index.

This table considers all factors that are involved in balancing water and makes recommendations for specific adjustments to bring the water into balance. A well-balanced pool has a reading of 0 on the saturation index. If the reading is negative, the water is likely to be corrosive; if it's positive, the water is likely to cause scaling.

TIP

SMART

Always adjust total alkalinity before you adjust pH, because once TA is in the proper range, the pH will be more stable, requiring only minimal adjustments.

IDEAL LEVELS

MEASUREMENT	OPTIMUM READING
Free chlorine	1.0 to 2.0 ppm
pH	7.2 to 7.8
Total alkalinity	80 to 125 ppm (for gunite) 125 to 150 (for vinyl, fiberglass, and painted plaster)
Total dissolved solids	Not to exceed 2,500 ppm
Calcium hardness	200 to 400 ppm

MAINTENANCE

FOR THE MOST PART, tending your pool or spa entails simple cleaning and upkeep. Sometimes, however, problems occur, ranging from murky water to noisy pumps. Often you'll be able to handle these situations on your own, but for some of the larger, more technical repairs you'll need professional help.

cleaning your
POOL

ALGAE BRUSH

Keeping the interior of your swimming pool fresh and clean doesn't demand intensive labor, but it does take a steady commitment. Expect to spend between 4 and 8 hours each week during the peak season—a small outlay compared with the amount of time you'll spend enjoying your pool.

THE BEST TOOLS FOR THE JOB

Using the right tools will make cleaning your pool easier and faster. You'll find these at any large pool-supply retailer.

LEAF SKIMMER This long-handled net is a must for removing large pieces of floating debris.

VACUUM Another weapon that is essential in any cleaning arsenal, a vacuum either connects to a pool's circulation system or has its own power supply. Vacuums suction out dirt that has settled to the bottom.

WALL AND FLOOR BRUSH This nylon-bristle brush cleans vinyl, fiberglass, and painted pools.

ALGAE BRUSH Concrete pools may require one of these; its stainless-steel bristles are up to the challenge of cleaning plaster walls.

TILE BRUSH If your pool has tiled walls, a handheld tile brush is great for removing calcium scale and other deposits without harming the grout. Use a pumice stone for stubborn spots.

TILE BRUSH

SKIMMING DEBRIS

Skimming by hand is one of the quickest and most effective ways to keep a pool clean. A few simple swipes will remove floating objects such as leaves before they sink to the bottom, greatly increasing the efficiency of the pool's circulation system and reducing the need for chlorine.

CLEANING OUT THE BASKETS

Keeping the strainer baskets clear will also boost the efficiency of the circulation system, resulting in a much cleaner pool. At least once a week, remove leaves and anything else that could

WALL AND
FLOOR BRUSH

The skimmer basket is located in the pool deck and traps floating debris. It needs to be cleaned out often—every day during periods of heavy use—to keep the pool filter functioning at maximum capacity.

obstruct the water flow, especially if your vacuum is connected to the mechanical skimmer. Strainer baskets may be in the pool deck or, for an above-ground pool, attached to the side.

VACUUMING

Vacuuming every week helps keep the water clear and reduces the need to add sanitizing chemicals. Vacuums come in many designs and styles (see page 98). All manual vacuums should be worked back and forth across the swimming pool, overlapping slightly on each stroke. Depending on the amount of dirt in the pool, it may be necessary to clean the filter each time you vacuum.

CLEANING THE WALLS

Brushing the pool walls at least once a week helps eliminate everything from calcium scale to algae buildup before serious problems develop. You can use a stiff brush on a plaster-lined concrete pool, but fiberglass and vinyl pools require a softer brush.

For tiles, be sure not to use anything too abrasive or stiff, as it can scratch the tiles or destroy the grout. Water-line tile scum can be removed with a non-abrasive chlorine-based liquid and a tile brush or a sponge. For tough spots, use a nylon scouring pad or a pumice stone, which works like a giant eraser. Always use a cleaner recommended by the pool manufacturer.

BEFORE THE FIRST SWIM

TEMPTING AS IT IS to plunge into your pool the moment construction is complete, you need to clean and balance the water first. New pools, whether fiberglass, vinyl lined, or concrete, invariably contain dust and other dirt that need to be eliminated. To do this, run the pool's filter continuously, 24 hours a day, until the water is clear. This may take anywhere from a day or two to an entire week or more. Periodically, you will need to stop and clear the filter (see pages 208–209) so the purification process will be successful.

Plaster-coated gunite and shotcrete pools pose an additional challenge: The wet plaster often turns the water murky. Handling this will require more time and will also require you to keep a closer eye on the filter, which will need more frequent cleaning. After the water is clear, reduce the filtration time by one hour a day until clarity is achieved. Then balance the pH, total alkalinity, and other factors of water chemistry (see pages 198–201). When the water is balanced, add a sanitizer such as chlorine and then start swimming.

cleaning your
SPA

Because of their exceedingly high water temperatures as well as the heavy use they get, spas tend to require frequent maintenance to keep them clean.

THE BEST TOOLS FOR THE JOB

The best tools for keeping a spa clean are basically the same as those used to clean swimming pools—just on a smaller scale.

LEAF SKIMMER As in a pool, this long-handled net is necessary for removing large pieces of floating debris.

VACUUM A spa vacuum can be powered in several ways. If your spa is not connected to the circulation system of an in-ground pool, a good solution is a vacuum powered by a jet of water from a garden hose.

SPA WAND A more streamlined alternative to a vacuum, a spa wand (right) also collects debris through suction. It may be powered either by your pumping or turning the handle or by a rechargeable battery. A spa wand is also handy for cleaning pool steps.

BUCKET AND SOFT SPONGE These two low-tech tools are a must for cleaning interior spa walls.

SKIMMING AND VACUUMING

Since a spa is so small, even a minimal amount of debris can lower the efficiency of the circulation system. Bring out the skimmer each time you use your spa. In addition, either vacuum or use a spa wand twice a week to remove litter that has settled to the bottom.

CLEANING OUT THE BASKETS

Debris-free baskets are essential to the proper operation of the circulation system. Clean the skimmers twice a week by removing leaves and anything else obstructing the water flow. With in-ground spas, the strainer baskets are hidden in the surrounding deck; for portable spas, the baskets are near the pump.

A spa may be smaller, but it requires just as much maintenance as a pool.

CLEANING
THE INNER SURFACE

Because total dissolved solids (see page 201) build up quickly, spa water needs to be drained fairly often. Emptying the spa provides an opportunity for cleaning the inner surfaces. Brush the spa interior to eliminate calcium scales and any algae buildup. A plaster-lined concrete spa can withstand stiff brushing, but fiberglass and acrylic spas are more delicate.

To clean tile, don't use anything very abrasive or stiff that could scratch the tile and destroy the grout. A pumice stone (above) works well, removing scale like a giant eraser. A putty knife is also great for scraping off especially heavy scale. Another alternative is to dissolve the scale with a 50-50 mix of water and muriatic acid. Apply it with a nylon brush and start scrubbing (see safety tip at right). Rinse well when you're finished.

TIP

SAFETY Muriatic acid is extremely corrosive, and its vapors can be toxic if inhaled. When working with this substance, be sure to protect your eyes and hands and work in a very well-ventilated area.

equipment
MAINTENANCE

Just like a pool or spa's shell, the mechanical equipment that keeps everything running efficiently will benefit from regular maintenance. Most of these chores are simple. If you perform them regularly, you'll be able to spot and handle small problems before they turn into big ones.

THE PUMP

The pump for a pool or spa requires very little maintenance. Pumps are generally self-priming—meaning they don't have to be filled with water before you turn them on at the start of the season. But you'll need to regularly clean out the strainer basket inside, in most cases once a week. To get to the basket, remove the top of the pump housing. Refer to the owner's manual to determine the specific location of your pump's basket.

While you're checking the basket, take a moment to inspect the condition of the O-ring or gasket that seals the lid of the pump housing. If it is cracked or has deteriorated, replace it. Otherwise, the lid won't be able to form the seal that's needed to keep the pump in operation.

Serious pump problems, such as an obvious water leak, will require professional help.

THE FILTER

No matter which type of filter you have in your pool or spa—cartridge, sand, or diatomaceous earth—it will need periodic cleaning to keep the water clear. Depending on the type of filter and how heavily you use your pool or spa, filter

Periodic care of a pool's mechanical equipment will keep everything running smoothly and head off potential problems before they arise.

cleaning frequency can range anywhere from once a month to three or four times each year.

Contrary to what you might expect, cleaning the filter more often than that doesn't help. In fact, it hinders the filtration process. That's because a slightly dirty filter is actually more efficient than a perfectly clean one. The particles of dirt lodged in it help trap additional particles, removing debris from the water more quickly.

Ideally, the filter should be cleaned before any deterioration in water quality is noticeable. To avoid having any problems, check the pressure gauge and the flow meter in the pool—one is positioned on the line into the filter, the other on the return line out of the filter. As the filter becomes dirty, the difference in flow between the gauges will increase. When the difference reaches 10 to 15 pounds per square inch, it's time to clean the filter. (See the chart at right for general cleaning advice; follow the manufacturer's instructions for more specifics.)

THE HEATER

Of all the equipment connected to a pool or spa, the heater requires the least maintenance. Gas heaters, for instance, can usually go for a year or two—sometimes longer—before they need professional servicing, and electric heaters can go longer still. With either type, check the manufacturer's recommendations.

If the heater doesn't warm up the water, calcium scales might be building up in its tubes, restricting the flow.

TIP

TIME

Two strainer baskets are better than one. Buy an extra and use them alternately. This will allow you to let the dirty basket dry out, making it easy to remove hair and other debris from it.

CLEANING THE FILTER

TYPE	FREQUENCY	TECHNIQUE
Cartridge	Every three to four months	Turn off the pump. Remove the filter, hose it off, and soak it in detergent according to the manufacturer's instructions for removing oils.
Sand	Every month	Turn off the pump. Circulate water through the filter in the reverse direction for about 10 minutes, a process known as backwashing.
Diatomaceous earth (D.E.)	Every three to four months	Turn off the pump. Backwash the filter (see above), then add more diatomaceous earth to the skimmers. Water will carry the D.E. to the filter and recoat it.

troubleshooting common
PROBLEMS

Even with diligent maintenance of your pool or spa, issues will occasionally arise. The problems listed below are among the most common. Most of them can be handled by homeowners.

POOL OR SPA SHELL

PROBLEM	POSSIBLE CAUSE	SOLUTION
Loss of grouting in tiled pools or spas	Soft water, which has low calcium levels and can sometimes dissolve the calcium in grouting	Regrout the pool and test the calcium levels in the water. If it's lower than 250 ppm, add calcium chloride.
Rough, scaly surfaces	Incorrect balance among pH, total alkalinity, and calcium hardness	Test for pH, total alkalinity, and calcium hardness and bring the levels within recommended parameters. A pool-supply store can conduct a Langelier water-balance test (see page 201) to advise you further.
Slippery surfaces	An algae colony, which may have formed because of insufficient chlorination or dead spots in water circulation	Use a brush on the slippery area to remove as much algae as possible, then superchlorinate (see page 195). An algicide may be needed to prevent a recurrence.
Tide mark at the water line	Buildup of greasy deposits, such as suntan lotion and cosmetics	Brush the area using a cleanser recommended by a pool-supply store; be sure it will not react with chlorine in the water.

WATER QUALITY

PROBLEM	POSSIBLE CAUSE	SOLUTION
Cloudy or milky water	Polluting residue from suntan lotion or other oils	Clean the skimmer baskets and filter, and operate the pump for a longer time. Superchlorinate the pool (see page 195), then add a clarifier, which causes suspended particles to settle.
	High pH, high alkalinity, or both	Test and adjust pH and total alkalinity.
Cloudy, greenish water	Low chlorine levels, which allow algae to colonize the pool or spa	Superchlorinate the water with chlorine—to 10 ppm if the water is only slightly green and to 25 ppm if the water is solid green. Also brush the interior walls to remove algae, and clean the filter to remove dead algae.
Rust-colored water	Steel or iron fittings that have corroded because of low pH	Replace any metal fittings with copper or plastic piping. Then drain or dilute the rust-colored water—contact your pool installer to find out how to do this safely. Remove any rust stains from pool surfaces with a tile-and-liner cleaner. Make sure the fresh water you add is properly balanced.
Eye or throat irritation	A too-acidic or too-alkaline pH	Test and correct pH. To lower it, add dry acid daily according to packaging instructions until the proper pH reading is obtained. To raise the pH, add soda ash in the same way.
	Too many chloramines in the water	Superchlorinate.
Bathers' blond or tinted hair turns green	High levels of copper in the pool, either from an algicide or from copper pipes corroding because of low pH	Check the pH and raise it if necessary. If too much algicide has been added, add more water to bring the pool or spa into balance.

FILTER AND PUMP

PROBLEM	POSSIBLE CAUSE	SOLUTION
Sudden decrease in water flow rate	Obstructions in the supply line, preventing water from being pulled into the pump	Shut the pump off immediately to prevent it from over-heating and burning out. Check for blockages in both the pump and the skimmer strainer baskets.
Pump runs but doesn't pump	Low water level in the pool; a clogged filter; damage to the impeller inside the pump; air leaks in intake lines	If the pump is hot, shut it off immediately to avoid burnout. Check the water level and add more water if needed. Check the filter and clean or replace it. If the pump still does not work, call a technician to check for impeller damage or air leaks.
Leaking pump	A deteriorated seal around the pump shaft	Replace the seal according to the instructions in the owner's manual.
Noisy pump	An oversized new pump, which is trying to discharge more water than is coming in; something jammed inside the impeller of an old pump	If the pump is oversized for the piping system (see pages 84–85), switch to a smaller pump. If the pump is an older one, check the impeller and remove any obstructions according to the owner's manual.

structural
REPAIRS

Although good swimming pools and spas are built to last, occasional mishaps can cause damage to the shell, requiring patching. In most cases, it's best to seek the assistance of a professional so that no additional damage is caused.

SEARCHING FOR LEAKS

Before you can repair a leak, you've got to find it. It's often difficult to determine whether a drop in the pool's water level is the result of a leak or normal evaporation. You can call in a professional leak detector to make the diagnosis, but first perform a "bucket test" yourself.

Fill a bucket three-quarters full with water and mark the water line on the inside of the bucket. Also mark the water line on the wall of the pool. Let the bucket float in the pool—with the handle removed for better stability—for two or three days, keeping swimmers away. If the water loss is due to evaporation, the water level in both the bucket and the pool will have gone down by the same amount. If it's due to a leak, the level of the pool will have dropped farther than the water in the bucket.

REPAIRING CRACKED CONCRETE

Just as with a basement wall or foundation, the concrete walls of a pool or spa can sometimes crack as the surrounding soil moves. Small cracks can be repaired easily, but larger ones may indicate

A bucket test can determine whether a pool is leaking. If water in the pool disappears faster than it evaporates from the bucket, this may be a sign of trouble.

structural problems that have to be corrected through excavation.

In general, a crack less than ¼ inch wide and shorter than 2 feet long can be repaired, although the process is time-consuming. The pool must first be drained to below the level of the crack, something that should not be done without a professional's guidance—a drained shell can crack further or pop out of the ground. After draining, use a chisel to widen the crack slightly and remove loose material from the edges.

Dampen the concrete and make a patching compound with portland cement. Then work the compound into the crack with a mason's trowel and brush the patch with muriatic acid to create a smooth texture (see safety tip on page 207). Coat the entire surface with an epoxy-based paint so the patched area or areas won't be visible.

REPLASTERING

Daily contact with chemicals and exposure to outdoor elements can slowly dissolve the plaster coating in a concrete pool and cause it to chip in a process known as spalling. Although this does not pose a structural hazard, it is unsightly and can create jagged edges that harbor algae. You can repair spalling by patching, but it will recur. Eventually, you'll need to replaster, usually within 7 to 10 years of the pool's construction. A plasterer will first sandblast off the old plaster to ensure that the new coat will adhere well.

RECOATING FIBERGLASS

Although fiberglass pools are extremely durable, their gelcoat surface may fade, turn dull, or stain. If the deterioration is limited to one small area, more gelcoat can be applied to that spot. But if the damage covers a large area, the pool may have to be drained and the entire shell recoated (draining should be done only under a professional's supervision). You can coat your fiberglass pool with epoxy paint instead of gelcoat to enhance its appearance.

ABOVE: A small crack in the wall of a concrete pool, such as the one shown above, can sometimes be corrected. If the crack is longer than 2 feet, however, this can indicate structural problems that cannot be resolved simply with patching.

ABOVE: To properly patch a small crack, drain the pool to below the level of the crack. In order to create a fresh edge for the patching material to adhere to, widen the crack with a chisel or other tool.

BELOW: Once the crack has been widened slightly, dampen the concrete and work a patching compound containing portland cement into the crack. After that, smooth the edges using a mason's trowel.

ABOVE: While large tears in a vinyl pool require that an entire new liner be installed, small tears such as the one above, measuring 3 inches or less, can be repaired.

TIP

SAFETY

In a vinyl-lined or fiberglass pool or spa, a bulge in the side may indicate either drainage or structural problems—both of which are major and will require excavation and possibly even replacement of the pool. If the bulge is sizable—more than 2 feet in diameter—immediately call the installer and don't swim in the pool until it's checked.

PATCHING A VINYL LINER

The lining of a vinyl pool can be torn easily, but small tears—less than 3 inches long—can also be repaired easily. In many cases, you can do it yourself rather than bring in a professional. Anything much longer than 3 inches may require replacing the entire liner.

The most common way to repair a torn vinyl liner is to drain the pool to just below the tear mark—being careful not to completely empty the pool, unless under a professional's supervision. Then patch the liner, similar to the way you patch a bicycle inner tube (see process at right). To make the repair, it is important to have a piece of material that is identical to the original pool material. To prepare for eventual patching needs, ask the installer to give you an extra piece of liner when the pool is constructed.

Some manufacturers make underwater patching kits. To use one of these kits, position the patch, then apply pressure from the center outward to squeeze out any water.

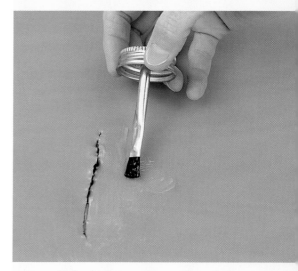

ABOVE: To begin the process, rough up the area with a piece of sandpaper. Then coat it with a solvent cement; also apply the cement to the back of the patch.

BELOW: Once the solvent cement has dried and become tacky, cut the patch so it extends at least 3 inches on all sides of the tear. Apply the patch.

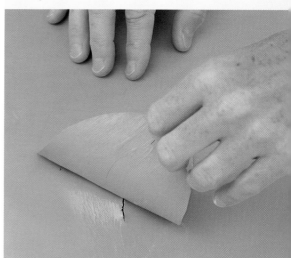

FROM SWIMMING POOL TO ICE-SKATING RINK

IF YOU LIVE IN AN AREA that has at least 2 months of temperatures below freezing, you may be able to have your in-ground swimming pool do double duty as an ice-skating rink. To transform it, winterize the pool (see opposite page), lowering the water level as described. Float a large vinyl liner on the water that extends onto the deck for about 2 to 3 feet and hold it in place with water-filled plastic jugs or sandbags. Fill the liner with water to a depth of at least 4 inches and allow it to freeze solid. Four or more inches of ice won't harm the pool at all.

seasonal
MAINTENANCE

WINTERIZING

If you live in an area that experiences freezing temperatures, you'll need to clear the water out of your pool's plumbing at the end of the swimming season. Frozen water won't harm the pool structure itself, but it can damage the pipes. Use an air compressor to blow water out of the lines, following the manufacturer's instructions. Also drain as much water as possible from the heater and filter. If any water remains, add nontoxic antifreeze—which differs from automotive anti-freeze and is available from pool-supply stores. Disconnect the pump and heater. Then disconnect, clean, and store any chemical feeders.

Thoroughly vacuum and clean the pool and empty the skimmer baskets. Close the valve on the skimmer line and lower the water level to about 18 inches below the coping. Superchlorinate to remove chloramines. Finally—and most important of all—tightly cover the pool or spa. This will keep debris from accumulating in the water, making it vastly easier to open the pool in the spring.

If you'll keep using your spa during the cold weather, just continue your regular maintenance. On days that are too cold for outdoor soaking, lower the thermostat but keep the circulation system running to prevent the pipes from freezing. In the event of a severe freeze, drain all the plumbing but leave the spa full.

OPENING FOR THE SEASON

If properly prepared for the winter, a pool or spa can be opened during the spring with minimum effort. The most essential step is to clean the surrounding area—hosing and sweeping dirt and debris away—before opening the cover. If you don't clean first, the winter's accumulation will empty into the pool.

Return the pool's water level to normal using a garden hose. Any equipment, such as the pump or heater, that was disconnected will need reconnecting. Open the valve on the skimmer line so that water flows through the circulation system again. When everything is functioning, balance the water by testing the pH and total alkalinity, then superchlorinate. Run the pump 24 hours a day, reducing the run by an hour or two each day until the water is perfectly balanced. This may take a week or more.

In warmer climates, seasonal pool maintenance is virtually nonexistent. However, in climates where water freezes, or where a pool or spa will remain dormant for long periods, you need to take proper care of your investment and make sure it's ready for use when warm weather returns.

SAFETY

ALONG WITH THE PLEASURE of owning a pool or spa comes a big responsibility: providing a safe environment for swimmers and non-swimmers alike. This means securing the area around the pool, encouraging responsible behavior, and providing constant supervision of children. Some safety measures may be mandated by your town's laws or by the terms of your insurance policy. Other crucial steps to ensure that your pool or spa remains a safe source of fun are up to you.

water
SMARTS

According to the U.S. Consumer Product Safety Commission, the vast majority of people who drown or suffer underwater injuries in a swimming pool are children under the age of 5. A young child can drown in less time than it takes to answer a telephone—or to read this sentence.

CHILD'S PLAY

Well-designed barriers can do quite a lot to keep children out of your pool area when no one is out there supervising (see pages 222–223), but even the most secure fence doesn't guarantee safety. The fact is most child drownings and submersion injuries occur in the presence of one or both parents. Fortunately, there are some steps you can take to ensure that your children and their pals can frolic to their hearts' content—and your peace of mind.

LEARNING TO SWIM If a pool figures in your future, make sure your youngsters learn to swim. The American Academy of Pediatrics recommends starting swim classes once your child reaches the age of 4. Many organizations, including the Red Cross, the YMCA, and the YWCA, offer reasonably priced swimming classes for young children.

If your toddlers take swimming lessons in the spring, chances are they'll be swimming like fish by summer's end. But they may forget their new skills if they don't have the opportunity to swim over the winter. So if you close your pool for the cold months, be sure to either take your youngsters to an indoor pool every couple

Water games can provide hours of fun for swimmers of all ages, but make sure you set rules for safe play—and see that everyone obeys them.

of weeks for practice sessions or sign them up for some refresher lessons the following spring.

DON'T COUNT ON TOYS Rafts, inner tubes, and inflatable animals can give your youngsters hours of fun in the water. And wearable flotation devices such as water wings and float suits can boost the confidence of budding swimmers. But never rely on these playthings as substitutes for serious safety equipment—and your own eagle-eyed attentiveness.

KEEP WATCH As most parents are well aware, small children are agile, fearless, and fast. But even older kids who are good swimmers should be watched carefully when they're in or near the pool. If you have to leave the area—even for a second or two—take the kids with you. When you have a pool party, arrange for designated watchers to supervise the children. Better yet, hire a professional lifeguard to be on duty.

BE PREPARED When a pool accident happens, a fast response is crucial. Be sure to learn water rescue techniques, artificial respiration, and cardiopulmonary resuscitation (CPR), and keep your skills up to date by taking refresher courses. Make sure that all babysitters, including grandparents and older siblings, do the same. (YMCA and YWCA lifeguard courses include all these rescue procedures.) In addi-

tion to other safety equipment (see page 221), keep a cordless or cellular telephone beside the pool, programmed with emergency numbers.

RULES FOR POOLS

When you own a pool or spa, setting a few simple rules can spell the difference between hours of nagging worry and countless days of pleasure and relaxation. Here are some guidelines to enforce:
- No running around the pool.
- No unsupervised children in or around the pool.
- No glass containers at poolside.
- No drinking alcohol while swimming.

(see page 221)

TIP

SAFETY ▷ A lightning strike can be deadly. Clear the pool at the first sound of thunder or if you know that a storm is close by, and do not let anyone go back into the water for at least 20 minutes after the last thunderclap.

DIVING DOS AND DON'TS

WHEN DIVING INTO THE WATER, DO:
- Plan your dive path. Know the shape and depth of the pool as well as the location of other swimmers and objects that are on or under the surface.
- Learn and practice proper diving techniques. Hold your head and arms up and steer with your hands. If you're using a board, dive straight ahead from the end, not off the side.
- Before you dive, bounce lightly on the board to check its spring.
- Aim for the surface. Shallow dives are the only safe kind to do in home pools. Deep vertical dives, like the ones competitive divers perform, require specially designed pools with very deep water throughout.
- Yield the right-of-way to swimmers already in the water.

TO AVOID INJURY, DON'T:
- Dive alone.
- Drink alcohol and dive.
- Dive into an above-ground pool.
- Dive into shallow water or across narrow parts of a pool.
- Play or roughhouse on the diving board.
- Try backflips or fancy dives.
- Dive through inner tubes or other floating objects.

around the POOL

Living next to any body of water poses certain risks. That's true even if your aquatic territory consists of a spa little bigger than a bathtub. In addition to installing nonslip decking (see pages 146–149) and adequate lighting (pages 178–181), following a few basic precautions will enhance safety.

HAZARDS TO ELIMINATE

When you put people and pools together, trouble can brew in a hurry. Here are some of the most common causes of problems, along with commonsense ways of avoiding them.

TOO MANY SWIMMERS Amid the noise and confusion of an overcrowded pool, a swimmer in distress can easily go unnoticed. In addition, the presence of a large, excited audience can encourage many children as well as some adults to show off and take dangerous chances. Limit the number of people that can be in the pool at any one time, and encourage rest periods.

CLUTTER Sports equipment and safety gear on the pool deck are tripping hazards, and toys present a double danger. Not only are they potential stumbling blocks, but, in or out of the pool, they are magnets for young children, who can easily fall into the water. Even furniture can pose risks. If a chair or a table is close to the edge, children may be tempted to use it as a diving board. Keep rescue equipment stowed in its proper place until it's needed. Put away

A pool deck that's open and free of clutter ensures safe passage for swimmers and non-swimmers alike.

toys, sports equipment, and other objects when they're not in use. Keep all furniture, planters, and accessories well away from the edge of the pool. Be sure the pool or spa cover is completely removed to prevent entrapment.

ELECTRICITY It's important to remember that electricity and water don't mix. Use only GFCI-protected receptacles around the pool or spa, and don't install any outlet within 10 feet of the water. Choose battery-operated appliances or electrical models that are approved for use outdoors and near water. And keep all appliances, including radios and CD players, far enough away that they can't fall or be pulled into the water. Don't touch any electrical appliance while you're wet, especially if you're in contact with something metal, such as a pool ladder. (It's OK to use a cellular or wireless phone while you're in a pool or spa, but never use a regular telephone.) If an appliance does

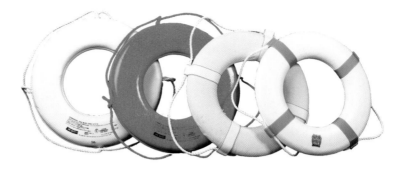

fall into the water, unplug it before you try to retrieve it. And always hire a qualified, licensed electrician to perform electrical repairs on pool or spa equipment.

POORLY MAINTAINED WATER Safe swimming demands clear, sanitary water. The water in your pool or spa should have the correct chemical balance, be free of any leaves and other debris, and be clear enough that you can see the bottom.

EQUIPPED FOR SAFETY

When trouble strikes, having basic rescue equipment at hand can make a big difference in your ability to respond. Pool-equipment suppliers and marinas sell a variety of devices that make it easier to reach swimmers in distress and pull them to safety. Whatever gear you choose, keep it easily accessible and ready to use. Inspect all pieces regularly and replace them at the first sign of wear and tear. Here are some must-haves:

SHEPHERD'S CROOK At 12 to 16 feet long, this pole extends your reach considerably. The half-circle at the end lets you draw in an unconscious person.

RESCUE TUBE This flexible vinyl-coated foam tube, often with a hook at one end, can be wrapped around a person. The attached nylon tow rope has a shoulder strap to make towing easier.

RING BUOY This classic piece of rescue equipment is designed to be thrown to a conscious person who can

hold on while being pulled to safety. Choose a buoy with a rope at least as long as half the width of your pool at its widest point. Or keep buoys on each side of the pool, with the line coiled and ready for use. Don't use an inner tube or other inflatable toy for a water rescue.

SAFE SLIDING

A water slide can provide hours of fun. But as with diving boards, it's crucial to follow basic safety procedures. Ask your contractor or pool technician to help choose the best model for your pool. Place the slide where water is deep enough so that people who use it won't hit their feet on the pool bottom, because leg fractures can result. But if you place the structure in very deep water, you'll want to restrict its use to good swimmers. Share these guidelines with all would-be sliders:

- If the slide does not empty into deep water, slide in a seated position, feet first. If the water is deep, sliders may safely go down lying flat, belly down, headfirst, or hands out in front.
- No one may use the slide as a diving board, no matter how securely it is fastened to the deck.
- Only one person at a time may use the slide.
- Swimmers already in the water have the right-of-way.
- No clowning around or roughhousing on the slide.

restricting
ACCESS

An unfenced, uncovered pool or spa is a tragedy waiting to happen. Most cities have laws requiring some sort of protective barrier. Even if your area has no fencing mandates and no neighbors for miles around, a fence or wall and a sturdy cover are the best safety investments you can make.

VERTICAL BARRIERS

The guidelines below, established by the U.S. Consumer Product Safety Commission (CPSC), are the minimum requirements for keeping young children from going over, under, or through a pool barrier. Legal requirements can differ by community, so check with your local building department before installing a fence or wall.

FENCES AND WALLS

- The barrier, whether a fence or wall, should completely surround the pool. If your house forms part of the barrier, the doors leading to the pool should have alarms in place, or the pool should have a power safety cover (see pages 96–97 and 224–225).

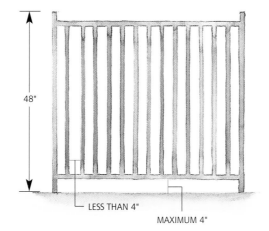

48"

LESS THAN 4"

MAXIMUM 4"

ABOVE: **For safety and privacy, nothing beats a tall wooden fence.**

OPPOSITE PAGE: **This red stucco wall acts as a safety barrier for the pool and adds color to the landscape.**

- The fence or wall should be at least 48 inches high, with no openings or projections (including crossbars) that a young child could use as a foothold or handhold.
- The bottom of the barrier should be no more than 4 inches above the ground on the side facing away from the pool.
- Vertical fence slats should be less than 4 inches apart.
- In a chain-link or lattice fence, no opening should be more than 1¾ inches wide.

GATES

- Gates should be self-closing and self-latching; they should close in the direction of the pool (so a child who pushes against an open gate will close it).
- If the latch-release mechanism is less than 54 inches from the bottom of the gate, it should be at least 3 inches below the top of the gate on the side facing the pool (thereby preventing a child from reaching over the top to spring the latch).
- Within 18 inches of the latch-release mechanism, no opening on the fence or gate should exceed ½ inch. This will prevent children from reaching small fingers through an opening to release the latch.

These plexiglas panels allow the homeowners to see the pool and ocean from the house but still keep children safely away.

LESS THAN ½"

MINIMUM 3"

ALARMS AND COVERS

When your house serves as part of the pool barrier, door alarms or a pool power safety cover is essential equipment. For extra insurance, install both (in some places the law requires it).

ALARMS The legal requirements regarding alarms differ from one community to the next. However, these are the minimum standards recommended by the CPSC:

- Every door leading to the pool area should be equipped with an alarm that sounds for at least 30 seconds whenever the door is opened.
- The alarm should be loud (at least 85 decibels when measured 10 feet away from the door) and distinct from other household sounds, such as telephones, doorbells, and smoke alarms.
- The alarm should have an automatic reset feature.
- To allow adults to pass through the door, the alarm should have a switch that deactivates the mechanism for up to 15 seconds. The switch should be installed at least 54 inches above the door's threshold.

SAFETY COVERS Don't confuse pool safety covers with covers that are designed simply to keep the water warm and free of debris. Such covers can be more hazardous than an uncovered pool, since a child (or pet) who falls or jumps onto a lightweight cover will cause it to collapse and may be trapped in the water-filled folds and drown. Whether you choose a motor-driven safety cover or one that you roll on and off using a hand crank, look for a cover that:

ABOVE: This safety net has openings that are too small for a child's head or body to fit through but too large for kids to walk on. It's useful when you want to allow safe access to the pool deck. The net can also be removed quickly when you're ready to swim.

RIGHT: A rigid spa cover that's intended to prevent accidental drownings should support about 400 pounds.

- Meets Standard F1346-91 of the American Society for Testing and Materials. Such a cover will support the weight of two adults and a child (roughly 400 pounds), thus permitting an easy rescue should someone fall onto it.
- Is made of tough mesh netting that lets water drain through. This is a crucial consideration, as a young child can drown in less than an inch of water.
- Has no gaps along the perimeter that a small child could crawl through.

SPA COVERS Spa covers are designed primarily to keep heat in and litter out. But if you have children or pets, make sure the barrier will support their weight, and yours, in the event of an accident. A spa cover should meet the same weight-bearing standards as a pool cover.

SECURING ABOVE-GROUND POOLS

A typical above-ground pool, whose sides reach up 48 inches or so, serves as its own barrier. Still, extra protection is always a good idea and may be mandated by local law. Deck kits made for above-ground pools usually include a 36-inch-high fence. Or you can purchase fencing from the pool's manufacturer and mount it on top of the pool wall. From the standpoint of a small child, that leaves only one possible point of entry to the pool: the stairs. To eliminate that weak link in your security system, either enclose the stairs with a fence and gate that meet the standards listed on page 223, or remove the stairs when the pool is not in use (see illustrations below).

With their raised sides, above-ground pools can foil even the most determined toddler. Still, it's best to go the extra mile and add a sturdy (and good-looking) fence.

BLOCKING ACCESS TO THE STAIRS KEEPS UNSUPERVISED CHILDREN OUT OF AN ABOVE-GROUND POOL.

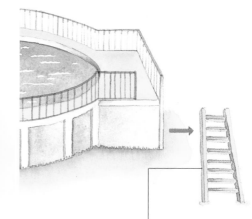

REMOVING THE STAIRS IS ANOTHER OPTION.

SAUNAS

FOR THOUSANDS OF YEARS, the sauna has been a place of both healthful relaxation and social recreation, and its appeal is growing. Thanks to new technology, you can install saunas indoors as well as out, and prepackaged kits make them eminently affordable.

the allure of the
SAUNA

Whereas swimming pools and spas let you experience the pleasure of bathing in water, saunas provide the physical and mental exhilaration of being bathed in heat. Not only are they sources of much-needed physical renewal, but they're also wonderful places for quiet contemplation.

With an eye toward design, a sauna can be as appealing on the outside as it is inviting on the inside.

FROM OUT OF THE PAST

Ancient Finland was the birthplace of the sauna, and modern-day Finland continues to enjoy it as a vital part of the culture. The traditional heat source is wood, which is burned to heat a pile of volcanic rocks inside a wooden room. When the fire dies down, the sauna is ready to be used. To create humidity, water is ladled over the rocks, which causes an explosion of steam to rise into the room. Because of the high heat, people don't usually linger long—after 5 to 10 minutes, they all head outdoors to take a dip in a cool pond or stream or to roll in the snow. Then they go back into the sauna, where they gently massage their skin with small bundles of birch twigs known as vihtas to stimulate circulation. After using the sauna, most bathers rest in order to cool down, then have a light snack called a saunapala.

BENEFITS TO YOUR HEALTH

Besides providing a pleasurable way to relax, saunas also stimulate circulation through the cycle of perspiration, rapid cooling, and rest. Perspiring heavily may help to clean clogged pores, resulting in skin with a healthier glow. Some people believe that saunas also help temporarily reduce muscular and nervous tension and may even heighten mental awareness. In addition, doctors sometimes prescribe spending time in a sauna for patients with arthritis or rheumatism, because the heat of the sauna can temporarily reduce inflammation in muscles and joints. Saunas can also provide temporary relief for the common cold by clearing uncomfortable sinus congestion. As with anything, however, moderation is essential when you are using a sauna. Read the cautions on page 233, and be sure to talk to your doctor if you have specific concerns or questions.

sauna
ANATOMY

WOODSTOVE

GAS STOVE

ELECTRIC STOVE

SAUNA ROOMS

The sauna room is an insulated wooden box, usually rectangular, that features two or three tiers of wooden benches for reclining. In most cases, the stove holds a load of special volcanic rock—often imported from Finnish quarries—that releases a gentle and even heat. The ideal ceiling height for a sauna is about 7 feet—tall enough for most people to stand comfortably yet low enough to limit the volume of space to be heated. The interior is paneled with unfinished wood, which will stay pleasingly warm to the touch, unlike metal or plastic.

SAUNA STOVES

Modern sauna stoves can be fueled by wood, gas, or electricity. Each has its advantages.

WOODSTOVES These traditional stoves are an excellent option, particularly for outdoor saunas, but they do require a steady supply of wood. Be aware that they're banned in many locations by local building codes.

GAS STOVES These stoves come in many styles, including those with elec-

tronic ignition, which is preferable to a pilot light. They heat up quickly, are relatively inexpensive to operate, and are a good option for homes already connected to a gas line.

ELECTRIC STOVES These are the most convenient, as well as the most popular, stoves. In most models, heating coils are located beneath the rocks. Be sure to get a model that allows you to splash water on the rocks, as wood and gas stoves do. The resulting steam is an essential element in a true Finnish-style heat bath.

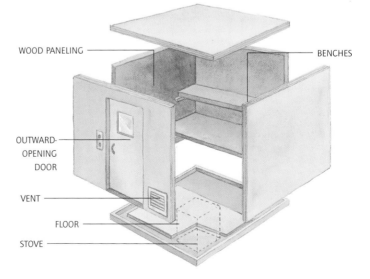

WOOD PANELING

BENCHES

OUTWARD-OPENING DOOR

VENT

FLOOR

STOVE

installing a
SAUNA

When you are choosing your sauna, size and shape are the two most important elements to consider. Saunas can be built from scratch or from a precut kit or prefabricated model.

LOCATING THE SAUNA

As with a swimming pool or spa, placing your sauna in the right location is essential to its success. If you choose to have it in your home, it's desirable to locate it near a dressing room as well as a bathroom with a shower. One popular location for saunas is a walk-in closet next to the master bathroom. Other options are out-of-the-way areas of the house, such as a corner of the basement, the attic, a spare bedroom, or even part of the garage.

If you prefer to have your sauna outdoors, you can install it in a cabana or pool house to take advantage of existing changing rooms or showers. If you don't have a pool, you can tuck the sauna into an unused area of the yard, which can be landscaped with trees and shrubs for additional privacy. When planning an outdoor sauna, remember to factor in the cost of site preparation, wiring, and any gas or electrical connections.

Whether it is indoors or out, allow 2 feet of bench space for each seated person (6 feet per person for reclining). For a single person, the smallest sauna would measure about 3 by 4 feet. A sauna for four people might measure 5 by 7 feet. A sauna approximately 8 by 10 feet could hold eight or nine people if benches were built on multiple levels.

BUILDING A CUSTOM SAUNA

If you're looking for a custom design, an experienced architect or a designer can create a unique sauna with a distinctive finish that will suit your particular space. Custom-designed saunas offer the greatest flexibility in terms of shape, bench layout, and materials and can be made to look like part of your house rather than a separate unit. As with all custom work, though, hiring a professional to design your sauna is the most expensive approach. Costs can range from a few thousand dollars to more than $10,000 for elaborate units.

MANUFACTURED SAUNAS

Far less expensive and easier to install than custom designs, manufactured saunas come in precut and prefabricated versions. Most manufacturers will make some custom modifications, such as a specific interior or exterior finish or a change in the dimensions or configuration of benches. Most precut kits include all the materials needed to construct a sauna, including the exterior roofing and siding for outdoor installations and precut tongue-and-groove lumber for the walls and ceilings. However, some manufacturers provide the materials for the interior only. In this case, you must build the framing according to instructions, as well as add insulation and provide a waterproof floor. Most manufacturers will supply the stove, although you may have to order it separately.

In addition to precut kits, prefabricated systems are also available. These are complete modular units, with finished interiors and exteriors, that are shipped in pieces and assembled easily. Wiring for lights is already in place, and electric stoves or heaters are usually included, though they'll need to be installed and connected by an electrician. Prefabricated saunas usually come in easy-to-handle packages, with their parts numbered to coordinate with step-by-step assembly instructions. Assembly usually requires only simple tools, such as a hammer and screwdriver, plus a coworker to help muscle everything into place.

Sauna costs vary greatly, but using a kit or a prefabricated system will usually save you money. A simple unit for one or two people might cost between $1,500 and $2,000. Larger units will cost considerably more. For instance, a sauna big enough to hold eight or nine people might cost $7,500 or more.

ABOVE LEFT: The first step in piecing together a sauna kit is to construct the outer frame. ABOVE RIGHT: Precut tongue-and-groove boards slide into position in the frame to form the sauna's walls and ceiling.

ABOVE LEFT: The door arrives prehung, which allows you to easily install its frame into one of the walls. ABOVE RIGHT: Once the sauna shell is pieced together correctly, each of the boards is nailed securely into place. BELOW: The roof can be added next. This is sometimes an extra item that is not included in a precut kit.

SMART TIP

For many people, the process of taking a sauna is an acquired taste. Before you buy a sauna, try one out not just once but several times to make sure you'll enjoy it.

231

enjoying your
SAUNA

A session in the sauna should be carefully choreographed to make the most of the sauna's benefits. Instead of squeezing your sojourn into a few spare minutes, try to spend a longer period in the heat and follow it with a cool-down and rest. Repeat the process several times for maximum effect.

CURING A NEW SAUNA

You'll need to properly cure a new sauna before taking your first heat bath. To begin the process, remove any construction debris or sawdust by sweeping the interior. Then vacuum and wipe the inside surfaces with a damp cloth. Also wash the heating rocks in the stove to keep any sand from ending up on the floor. The first time you turn on the stove, let it run for 30 minutes with the door open. This will help vent any noxious odors that result when protective coatings on the stove burn off. After half an hour, close the door and set the temperature as high as possible —usually about 200 degrees—and leave it that way for five or six hours. At that point the sauna is ready to use, and you can adjust the temperature to where you like it.

USING YOUR SAUNA

Following the traditional sequence of bathing in heat and then cooling down can accentuate the sauna experience. To begin, warm up the sauna. Most electric saunas take about 30 minutes to reach their full heat, which is between

With minimal maintenance, such as leaving the door open to cool down and dry out the inside after use, a sauna can remain fresh-looking even after years of steady use.

150 and 195 degrees. Before you step in, take a quick shower, then enter and sit or recline on a bench. At first, the humidity in the sauna will be low— about 5 to 10 percent—but it will gradually increase as you as you perspire. You can also increase the humidity by ladling water over the hot rocks, which produces a burst of steam. The steam will greatly heighten the effect of the heat and also increase perspiration.

When you leave the sauna, cool down by taking a shower or a quick swim. Some people enjoy having a brief rest before returning to the sauna. If that's your preference, lie down for approximately the same amount of time as you spent in the sauna. After cooling down or resting, head back to the sauna and repeat the entire process two or three times. End the final heat bath with a gentle loofah scrub—the modern equivalent of massaging with vihtas—then have a rest followed by a light snack.

SAUNA MAINTENANCE

Saunas, unlike swimming pools and spas, require very little maintenance. After using your sauna, turn off the stove and open the door to allow the wood surfaces to dry thoroughly. Wash the inside of the sauna every few months with a damp cloth and a cleanser or disinfectant recommended by the manufacturer. Electric and gas stoves need little if any maintenance, while woodstoves require occasional soot removal as recommended by the manufacturer.

Attention to location and layout will increase a sauna's desirability. This sauna benefits from being located next to a shower used for cool-downs.

resources

ASSOCIATIONS

National Spa & Pool Institute
2111 Eisenhower Ave.
Alexandria, VA 22314
703-838-0083
www.nspi.org

National Swimming Pool Foundation
224 East Cheyenne Mountain Blvd.
Colorado Springs, CO 80906
719-540-9119
www.nspf.com

POOLS

Delair Group
8600 River Rd.
Delair, NJ 08110
800-235-0185
www.delairgroup.com
Above-ground pools, fences

Paco Pools & Spas
784 Merrick Rd.
Baldwin, NY 11510
516-546-1400
www.pacopoolsandspas.com
*Vinyl-lined and gunite pools,
pool chemicals*

Raynor Pools
1460 Montank Hwy.
East Patchogue, NY 11772-5300
866-472-9667
www.raynorpools.com
*Vinyl-lined pools; heater, pump,
and filter parts; covers*

San Juan Pools
West Coast:
850 North Davidson St.
Eloy, AZ 85231
866-535-7946
East Coast:
2302 Lasso Lane
Lakeland, FL 33801
800-535-7946
www.sanjuanpools.com
Fiberglass pools and equipment

Swimmingpool.com
877-407-POOL
www.swimmingpool.com
*A wholesaler whose web site offers
a directory of in-ground pool
installers, above-ground pool dealers,
and equipment dealers.*

Viking Pools
800-854-7665
www.vikingpools.net
Fiberglass pools

PORTABLE SPAS, HOT TUBS, SAUNAS

Aqua Swim 'N' Spa
P.O. Box 3707
Brownsville, TX 78523
956-831-2715
www.rioplastics.com
Swim spas, physiotherapy spas

Callaway Woodworks
11320-A FM 529
Houston, TX 77041
877-518-9698
www.callawaywoodworks.com
Hot tubs, saunas, accessories

Dimension One Spas
2611 Business Park Dr.
Vista, CA 92081
800-345-7727
www.d1spas.com
Portable spas

Finlandia Sauna Products, Inc.
14010-B S.W. 72nd Ave.
Portland, OR 97224-0088
800-354-3342
www.finlandiasauna.com
Finnish saunas and accessories

Northern Lights Cedar Tubs
4122 Henderson Hwy.
Winnipeg, Manitoba
R2E 1B3 Canada
800-759-8990
www.cedartubs.com
Cedar hot tubs and saunas

Saunafin
115 Bowes Rd., #2
Concord, Ontario
L4K 1H7 Canada
800-387-7029
www.saunafin.com
*Sauna kits, prefab saunas,
accessories*

SwimEx, Inc.
373 Market St.
Warren, RI 02885-0328
800-877-7946
www.swimex.com
*Swim spas, aquatic therapy pools,
water exercise equipment*

MECHANICAL
EQUIPMENT

Hayward Pool Products
900 Fairmount Ave.
Elizabeth, NJ 07207
908-351-5400
www.haywardnet.com
Filters, valves, heaters, pumps, cleaners

Heliocol
800-79-SOLAR
www.heliocol.com
Solar pool heating

Pentair Pool Products
East Coast:
1620 Hawkins Ave.
Sanford, NC 27330
800-831-7133
West Coast:
10951 W. Los Angeles Ave.
Moorpark, CA 93021
800-831-7133
www.pentairpool.com
Pumps, heaters, filters, lighting

Raypak
2151 Eastman Ave.
Oxnard, CA 93030
805-278-5300
www.raypak.com
Pool and spa heaters

Solar Living
P.O. Box 12
Netcong, NJ 07857
973-691-8483
www.capturethesun.com
Solar-pool heating

CLEANING AND
MAINTENANCE

AquaChek
P.O. Box 4659
Elkhart, IN 46514-0659
574-262-2060
www.aquachek.com
Test strips and kits

Floatron
P.O. Box 51000
Phoenix, AZ 85076

480-345-2222
www.floatron.com
Solar-powered ionizer

Polaris Pool Systems
2620 Commerce Way
Vista, CA 92081-8438
800-822-7933
www.polarispool.com
*Automatic cleaners, chlorinators,
accessories*

Recreation Supply Co.
P.O. Box 2757
Bismarck, ND 58502-2757
800-437-8072
www.recsupply.com
*Water testing, pool cleaners,
leaf skimmers*

Specialty Pool Products
110 Main St.
Broad Brook, CT 06016-0388
800-983-7665
www.poolproducts.com
*Cleaners, spa covers, heaters,
filters, lighting*

ACCESSORIES

All-Safe
648 N. Eckhoff Street
Orange, CA 92868
800-786-8110
www.allsafepool.com
*Pool fences, safety net pool covers,
mesh pool covers, and automatic
pool covers*

Cover Pools, Inc.
800-447-2838
www.coverpools.com
Safety, solar, and automatic covers

Inter-fab
3050 S. Alvernon Way
Tucson, AZ 85713
800-737-5386
www.inter-fab.com
*Pool slides, diving boards, ball
games, and pool rails*

Katchakid
1737 Stebbins Dr., #220
Houston, TX 77043
888-552-8242
www.katchakid.com
Child safety-net cover

Recreation Supply Co.
(see Cleaning and Maintenance)
*Water sports, safety and rescue
equipment, lighting, handrails,
ladders, slides*

Recreonics
4200 Schmitt Ave.
Louisville, KY 40213
800-428-3254
www.recreonics.com
Pool lifts, ramps, aquatic wheelchairs

Smith and Hawken
800-940-1170
www.smithandhawken.com
*Outdoor furniture, umbrellas,
and accessories*

S.R. Smith
P.O. Box 400
Canby, OR 97013
800-824-4387
www.srsmith.com
Slides, diving boards, ladders, rails

Water Gear
P.O. Box 759
Pismo Beach, CA 93448-0759
800-794-6432
www.watergear.com
*Water toys, flotation aids, water
games*

LIGHTING AND LANDSCAPING

Cabana Village, LLC
501 Silverside Rd., #105
Wilmington, DE 19809
800-959-3808
www.cabanavillage.com
Sheds, pool houses, spa enclosures

Fiberstars, Inc.
44259 Nobel Dr.
Fremont, CA 94538
800-327-7877
www.fiberstars.com
Fiber-optic lighting

Trex
800-289-8739
www.trex.com
*Decking and railing made of
recycled plastic and wood*

credits

PHOTOGRAPHY

Top (T), Bottom (B), Middle (M),
Left (L), Right (R)

235; **Hester + Hardaway:** 192; **Saxon Holt:** 136L, 147, 176, 216, 224R; **D. A. Horchner/Design Workshop:** 1, 2T, 4T, 11, 17B, 41B, 72, 75T, 77B, 134, 149T, 154, 156R; **J.-C. Hurni:** 63T, 64, 65, 113T, 116B; **Courtesy of Inter-fab:** 100; **Rene Klein:** 78B, 110, 111T, 11T; **Mark David Levine:** 104L; **Terrence Moore:** 119B; **Jerry Pavia:** 111B; **Courtesy of Pentair Pool Products:** 82T, 85B, 88BL, 98, 103TL; **Robert Perron:** 85T; **Norm Plate:** 17T, 28, 42B, 190BL; **Courtesy of Polaris Pool Systems:** 99TL, 99TR; **Courtesy of Raynor Pools, Inc:** 121; **Courtesy of Recreational Supply Co.:** 221T; **Lisa Romerein:** 21T, 22T, 22B, 24B, 25, 29T, 29B, 33T, 38, 41T, 46, 53M, 55T, 59, 132–133, 151T, 160T, 160B, 170B, 173T, 174, 175B, 178, 182B, 183L, 184, 186T, 187T, 188T, 188BL, 188BR, 191T, 191B, 200T, 203B, 207T; **Susan A. Roth:** 95T, 117B, 120, 141, 149B, 164, 175TR; **Sam + Yvonne/Jupiter Images:** 77R, 104R; **Jeremy Samuelson:** 103TR; **Jeremy Samuelson/Jupiter Images:** 84, 86, 234; **Courtesy of San Juan Pools:** 123; **Courtesy of Saunafin:** 231TL, 231TR, 231ML, 231MR, 231B; **Courtesy of SCP Pool Corporation (photo by M. Thomas Blake):** 217B, 225; **Courtesy of S.R. Smith:** 101B; **Courtesy of Smith and Hawken:** 183R; **Thomas J. Story:** 165R, 218; **Courtesy of Strebel:** 31L; **Tim Street-Porter:** 10B, 12T, 12B, 16B, 35, 43T, 50, 52, 68, 73R, 102B, 175TL; **Tim Street-Porter/Beateworks/Corbis:** 7T, 60; **Courtesy of SwimEx:** 75B; **Courtesy of Viking Pools:** 61B, 113B, 122; **Dominique Vorillon:** 16T, 32, 34, 44T, 71T, 76, 148R, 173B, 179B, 202; **Dominique Vorillon/Jupiter Images:** 81; **Roger Wade:** 40, 67, 73L, 74B, 137T, 233; **Lee Anne White:** 13B, 18B, 19B, 23T, 23B, 24T, 26, 27TR, 66, 74T, 194, 210, 217T, 222

DESIGN

Arentz Landscape Architects: 56R, 130T, 158T, 193B; Authentic Provence: 20R, 203T; Shari Bashin-Sullivan/Enchanting Planting: 216, 224R; Tina Beebe & Buzz Yudell: 24B, 170B, 185B; Benedikt Strebel Tile: 31L, 119T; Corey Brooks/Design Workshop: 72; Jack Chandler Design: 186B; Steve Chase: 3B, 143B; Robert C. Chesnut: 8B, 168B; Yunghi Choi, Landscape Architect: 151B; Bob Clark Design: 15B, 20L, 69B; Tim Clarke, Inc.: 173B; Jim Clarke, Inc.: 71T; Russ Cletta: 29T, 174, 187T, 203B; Todd Cole Designs: 99B; Peter Cummin & Associates, Inc., Landscape Architects: 177BL; DeLellis Construction: 32; Dickson DeMarche, Landscape Architect: 130B, 138, 159T; Delaney/SEAM Studio: 145; Desert Sage Builders: 23B; Donaroma's Nursery: 2B, 33B; Nancy Driscoll: 147; Mary Effron Landscape Design: 108; Steven Erlich Architects: 10B, 43T; Kathy Fleming: 117B, 141, 175TR; Jamie Fogle/Design Workshop: 11, 149T; Cevan Forristt Landscape Design: 4B, 58, 190BL; Ray Forsum: 135T, 135B; Four Dimensions Landscape Development: 26; Fung + Blatt Architects: 35; Daniel J. Goss & Associates: 16T; Ann Clark Holt Design: 5B, 226; Honka Log Homes: 233; J.-C. Hurni: 113T, 116B; Mark Hutker & Associates, Architects, and Stephen Stimson, Landscape Architect: 93T; Ibarra-Rosano Design Architects: 179B; J.C. Enterprise Services: 19B, 74T, 66; Raymond Jungles, Landscape Architect: 7B, 18T, 36T, 49, 53B, 70, 144 (with Deborah Yates), 167B; Mia Lehrer & Associates: 13T, 83; Mark David Levine: 104L; Lewis Scully Gionet, Landscape Architects: 31R; Luis Llenza Garden Design: 23T, 24T; Laurie Lewis Design: 22B, 132–133, 160T, 173T, 182B, 188T, 188BL; Marmol Radziner & Associates: 46; Peter Magee, Builder: 28; Magrane Associates: 140; Tom Mannion Landscape Design: 61T, 129T, 131B, 156L; Joseph Marek, Landscape Architect: 160B, 175B, 207T; Steve Martino Associates: 56L, 172R; McLaughlin & Associates Architects: 137T; Carla Melson: 41T, 151T; Jeff Mendoza: 164; Manolo Mestre: 12B; Montana Log Homes: 40; Moonlight Basin: 74B; Natural Settings Pools, Spas and Water Features: 44T; Mario Navarro: 14B; Martyn Lawrence Bullard: 102B; Robert Liang Roof: 71B; Richard Neutra, Architect and Ted Russell, Designer: 16B; Carrie Nimmer: 217T; Robert Norris: 210; Don Nulty, Architect and Heide Baldwin, Landscape Designer: 25; W. Nydegger: 64; Oehme van Sweden & Associates: 6, 9T, 14T, 53T, 54B, 158B, 177BR, 193T; Outdoor Illuminations: 21B; Ben Page & Assoc.: 95T; Tom Pellet: 149B; Plimpton Associates: 101T; Containers by Red Trowel Gardens: 27M; Reisinger Rigging: 172L; Suzanne Rheinstein & Associates: 50; Suzanne Richman/Design Workshop: 75T; Sanchez & Maddux, Inc., Landscape Architects: 10T, 57T, 109T, 129B; Richard Shaw/Design Workshop: 4T, 17B, 41B, 77B, 154; Susan Sawicki: 120; Ahmed Smili: 187B; Michael Smith: 178, 183L; Scott Soden: 118B; Rob Steiner: 29B, 33T, 59; David Stevens: 92; Stephen Stimson Associates: 220; Studio Waterman, Inc.: 73L; John Suarez/Design Workshop: 1 (with Deanna Weber), 134; Jaska Tarkka: 233; Rose Tarlow: 7T, 60; Clyde Timmons/DesignWorks & Roger Good, Cloverleaf. Architects: Thomas & Denzinger: 30, 148L; Town & Country Cedar Homes: 67; Bernard Trainor Design: 9B, 190T; Michael Trapp: 15T; Tucker & Marks: 114; Urban Earth Design: 17T; Watercolors: 13B; Roger Waynick: 111B; Sheila Wertimer, Landscape Architect/Beth and David Simmons: 19T, 36B, 153T, 165L; Nick Williams and Associates: 69T; Chris Winters: 42B

index